Living with Awareness

Book 1

DANCE OF THE PYRAMIDS

A Personal Recipe to Aware, Enriched Living and Character

By Nalli

Mike Nally, Ph.D.
Dami Institute, Inc.
623 Whispering Pines Lane, Suite 2
P.O. Box 611
Coeur d'Alene, ID 83816-0611
Telephone: (208)676-8126

Cover design and illustrations by Drake Brodahl.
Back cover photograph taken by Paul Nally at Restland Cemetery, Dallas, Texas.

ISBN: 0-75961-286-2

This book is printed on acid free paper.

1stBooks - rev. 12/28/00

The Ingredients:

Writer's Preface 1

Dedication Message 6

Mind-Set Warm-Up: Let's Get Acquainted 7

Relationship: Its X's And Its O's 10

Sharing = Creating Value With Others and Nature 29

What Is Friendship? 46

Self: Who Am I? What Am I? 50

Denial, Deception, and Distraction are the Filters for a Blurred
Awareness 63

What's Context? 69

Communicative Relating: What's In A Word? 81

Listening and Silence 87

Questions and Answers: To be Aware of Them, Is To Be. 88

What is the Purpose of Sex? 98

Productive Activity: The Pretty Work of Aware Learning, Doing,
Teaching 104

Situational - Contextual Awareness (Common Sense Strikes Again, and
Again, and Again) 111

Humor A La Mode 122

WRITER'S PREFACE

The ideas presented in this book have been companions of mine for a number of years. This book's frame comprises notes taken from lengthy and diverse discussions with self and friends, real and imaginary (including a core group of contributors I call "The Gang in the Sky"). My daily strolls and fugue states are personally enriching because all forms of reality are welcome.

As the aware person quickly comes to notice, there is always a fresh crossroad at hand in life's journey. These choice points of potential joy or distress can be simple or complex, dreams or nightmares, paths to lush gardens or to graveyards of row upon row of stark crosses. Some paths are well-travelled, broad avenues of social cooperation, while others are vague and step-tricky, narrow lanes of dark selfishness. How is one to know?

This book is a guide for achieving creative balance, harmony, and peace with self, others, and Nature. The best-case, recommended remedies for the recurring briars, dilemmas, and distresses in living are: Relating and sharing, which translate behaviorally as creating opportunity and creating social value. When relating and sharing are actively expressed with respect, patience, productive activity and humor the situational-context of your awareness can be one of creative joy, not one of pain and sorrow.

I think of the concepts in this book as worded melodies. Melodies motivated by the familiar foursome of creative activities and well-being: namely, self-understanding, relationship development, values coopting, and personality enrichment. To me, the art-form of pursuing this "foursome" is the prime-time, humorous mystery in living. When fear, loneliness, and pollution, the "terrible trio", the major obstacles to all that is "good" in human potential, dominate our experiences we create war with self, others, and Nature. We strike living such a blow that it becomes chaotic and stress-fretten. It is easy to become lost when a person is without calming references and is cast-out.

Herein I join the reader in exploring, aided by a glowing lantern of hope rather than confused by the shadows of despair, the humorous and mysterious maze of self and future. Have you ever noticed how you, as the reader, help create the book? I believe the creative joining of a writer and a reader is a pathway of "purest ray." This blending of selves is timeless and magical. For example, a long-dead writer can reach across the ages simply by a sentence being read. Past becomes present, and magically times merge. Hey, let's party!

So then,.. why this book now? There are two primary reasons. 1) As the world turns, I don't like the mood that I sense forming all around it, and 2) each tick of the clock puts me that much closer to the "ashes to ashes, and dust to dust" leg of my personal journey. "Now", at one time, was my future... and I'm here.

We are all cooks in the same creative kitchen. We are all dancers at the same contextual party. We are all builders of our personal pyramids in the same warp-speed time-space. While none of us had any voice or vote about being beamed aboard this spaceship Earth, we do have collective authority about the physical condition and social manner of our living planet while we're here. I am not interested in being a victim in the "sheeple" herd, nor of existing embroiled in trivial enthusiasms and neurotic episodes. I don't want "off" the planet, I want to join other invested people in the marvelous adventure of "fixing" the planet and in creating a productively active human community. I hold no affection for selfish pessimism. A primary goal of mine is learning how to leave the planet better than I found her. A good place to start is with self... in all its aspects... in living context.

This book is my first "uff da" lantern to be run up the welcome pole as a signal to others of my presence, my interests, my thoughts, my intentions, and my invitation. I seek companionship with honest, tough-minded debater-doers who will strive to create social cooperation and global well-being. As my Papa Pal used to say, "If you aren't going to dream BIG,.. why bother to dream at all?"

Therefore, if we are to have the good fortune to create balance, harmony and peace, if we are to have any chance to plot our mutual future courses toward life, liberty and the pursuit of happiness, we must enter the 21st Century aware of the interacting roles of self, others, and Nature. The turmoil of this decade (the 90's) and the human challenge for the 21st Century are clear and undeniable. The Q is: **who** and **when**? The A is: **us** and **now**! Let us join our hearts, our hands, and our minds in the productive activity of creating the joy of living through aware relating and sharing. Let **us** begin **now**!

Author's comment: How came this book's title to be? Not easily, I assure you. We almost needed referees. My first title had about 23 1/2 words in it-- "Poetic, but too long," said some. I agreed. I shifted to a briefer "working" title of A Recipe for Relationship--"Too flat," said others. But I had grown fond of my "recipe" for blending ideas and for the things it let me do with the multiple aspects of self, context, and awareness. So I've tried to keep the flavor while losing the title.

The next "mind-wrestling" title episode came while on a trip to California with my friend Dave Martin (we can blame him). He and I knocked-about some title possibilities. Some critics think exhaustion won. Without admitting to anything stronger than coffee being involved, the title Dance of the Pyramids was born. Immediately upon hearing it, my brother Don said, "I don't get it." Of course, being a bi-athlete bicyclist, he would probably prefer <u>Tour of the Pyramids</u>. Some of his submitted suggestions were great fun with terrific graphics potential, but too politically tweaking for this book, at this time. Give me a few years.

Another long-time friend, Dr. Xu, thought <u>The Nally Touch</u> would be nice, with any workshops being called: "The Monk (me) and the Jimbo (him) Show." Give me a few years on these, too. The helpful suggestions and the critic's chirping go on late into the night. But I've chosen, and I hope "you <u>do</u> get it."

What influenced me to go with <u>Dance of the Pyramids</u>? Dance is my verb, pyramid is my noun. I think in these words, self-talk in these words, and I use them often. You'll see them in the book,.. perhaps more than you care to. To dance, for me, means "with others" usually. Havelock Ellis, in his <u>The Dance of Life</u>, said, "Dancing is the loftiest, the most moving, the most beautiful of the arts, because it is no mere translation or abstraction from life, it is life itself." Nicely put, very nicely, but I sense that Mr. Ellis has never been witness to a K-Mart "Sock Hop" special. I wonder if he knows which came first--the dance, or the music? Whoops, I'm drifting--whoa!

And the pyramid, the old tetrahedron, has been a <u>solid</u> favorite of mine for a lifetime of years. Many people, down through the ages, have enjoyed using the structure of the pyramid as a symbol for life and personality. In building one's life and personality, as in building a pyramid, to go higher you are well-advised to broaden your base. But not forever, for to spend all your time on the base is to build a platform, not a pyramid. Along with the horizontal, a little vertical is nice, and a little diagonal, now and then, that helps, too. To forget the angles in a pyramid is as to forget the seasoning in the soup. In both cases, you end up with "flat", for crying out loud. Ha! "For crying out loud" was one of my dad's frequent expressions.... Popular with his generation. An expression that is a bell-tone reminder to me of him whenever I hear it, read it, or think it. A block in my pyramid. For crying out loud, Dad, how ya' doing?

The eagle is, of course, a symbol used and admired by many since the gray dawn of human existence. I'm in that group of admirers, and I plan to "give you the bird" on any and all book covers that I am fortunate enough to get in print and color. The eagle is a constant in my "motive bank"--representing to me: grace, skill, independence, beauty, and grandeur. The soaring eagle and the grounded pyramid are the symbolic anchors at the extremes of my frolicking imagination, hypergolic mind-set and super-glue tenacity.

Over the years, being of human digestive linkage and unable to readily process raw grasses, I have come to appreciate good cooking. I have, in fact, become interested in the basic chemistry of cooking. Combining this "kneading" interest with my long-time fascination in the theories of personality development the model of an interactive "recipe" is, for me, a natural mix. My recipe notions are personal guides to daily creative exercises, games, and rhythm setting. But only guides, mind you, not prison chain-gang shuffles or chants of dull monotony. My motive currents are: 1) the building of a personal pyramid of balanced sweat and smiles, and 2) creating a romantic-dance souffle' in whatever "wok" I find myself. I want my outcomes to be as delight-filled and as biodegradable as wit and wisdom permit.

In writing these pages, as I move between my verb (dance) and my noun (pyramid), each "gotcha" and "colon-spin" is an attempt to share a glimpse of motive (an eagle) with you. While practice may not make my efforts hatch "perfect" it certainly makes "better" a happy possibility. So using a melted-down line from Robert Frost, I chase my foul-balls and re-tee my purpose with the determined thought: "I have books to write before I sleep." If only I knew more tales. Has anyone rafted the perilous, plunging River Styx lately? What, do you suppose, would such a trip reveal about the dehydrating nature of the obvious? Has anyone checked it out? Ah, "Once upon a time" my favorite opening to awareness-adventures.... And "Row, Row, Row your Boat" is another good one.

It was Socrates who said, "The unexamined life is not worth living." The masses have been quick to shout back at him during their numbing fall into despair's pit, "What do you know, anyway?" Across time and people, "desperation" has resonated at a broad range of decibels and frequencies... much the same as "prayer" has. It is, indeed, Mr. Socrates, awareness which serves as the critical element in blending a recipe for relationship, and in creating a dance of pyramids. The long recommended "twist and turn" for sorting the endless parade of dances crowding our daily affairs are: relating and sharing. When actively expressed with respect, patience, productive activity, and humor, your flowing context becomes a present of creative joy, not a past and future of care and woe. As a waltz can be joy's pairing, a boogie-woogie can get your joints to jumpin'.

This book is an invitation to both writer and reader to bring us to stroll together, in real and imagined ways, the special path of creating personal, social, and ecological awareness and will. Now, if only Mr. Socrates would telephone my brother and tell him--"Just as every life should be examined, every pyramid waxes happy when dancing,.. folla?"

My recipe for relationship is generic. As, for example, a recipe for pie in which you, as the creator, decide on the flavor, the size, and how much rhubarb, if any. I'm an optimist about community and living, in spite of my stress-scars. I even believe that Americans can, someday, master the metric system. This, some of my associates tell me, makes me a pigeon-toed optimist--one of strange gait and little speed.

So now,.. why have I told you all this? I'm not sure that I know, completely. Perhaps, so you won't cast stones at my "uff da" lantern, as it waves in the winds of night; or perhaps, so you will feel that you know me well enough to smile or frown freely across time and space to me as you greet these words. I invite you to my quest. Please, send me stories of personal choice points and creative moments in relating and sharing. My context awaits you. Welcome!

Aside #1: I like my recipe and I like how I have presented it in the following chapters. However, I hope that I will be able to add some "visual flavor" to this effort by the time you taste of it. At least one illustration or cartoon per section would be nice, I think.

Aside #2: Nalli is the original spelling of my Italian family name. My Italian grandfather "Jesse" changed Nalli to Nally upon entering this country in the late 1800's. In honor of simplicity and roots, I choose Nalli for my forum "circle name." My rooted, but not so simple, system and street names and title are: Michael Joseph Vitalis (Palkovic) Nally, Ph.D. Palkovic was my full-blooded Czech mother's birthname: Irene Elizabeth Angela "Pal" Palkovic. The Michael Joseph Vitalis Nally come to me from my father: Vitalis Michael Joseph "Vee" Nally. Besides the thick Italian lineage fiber, he graced me, via his mother Ina, with strands of English, Scottish, Tuscarora, and, it is wagged, a few gene-beans from ancient extra-terrestrial sojourners who stopped in the W. Va hills for some minor repairs and a little partying. The Ph.D., depending upon the source and hour of the night, can be translated as anything from Paid His/Her Dues, to Doctor of Philosophy, to Post Hole Digger. Your choice. But just call me Nalli.

Dedication Message

Relationships: Real and Unreal with Self and Unself

I dedicate this book to Carissa, Pam, and Tess; to persistence, patience, and a belief in the impossible; to Uncles Remus and Wiggly, and to lil' 'tar Laura.

As with many writers, I write about those special things which I hope to create in my own living adventure. Some of them, at times, seem rare, at times, impossible. But a little impossibility? You shouldn't let that stop you.

As the Queen (in Lewis Carroll's <u>Through the Looking Glass</u>, "Wool and Water", p.174) told Alice when Alice laughed and said, "There's no use trying, one can't believe impossible things."

"I daresay you haven't had much practice," said the Queen. "When I was your age, I always did it half-an-hour a day. Why, sometimes I've believed as many as six impossible things before breakfast."

A nod of warm regard to my high school mates, and especially to football-team co-captain Bill Jacobs. May a gentle wind caress their flights.

Mind-Set Warm-up: Let's Get Acquainted

Welcome to my kitchen. Please, come in. How are you? How are you really? Three major problems in living, for most of us, are fear, loneliness, and pollution. The best-choice remedy: relating and sharing with self, others and Nature.

My purpose in writing this book is to suggest ideas for improving personal and interpersonal relationships which may provide the reader with a fresh perspective in greeting his/her daily successes and setbacks. My intention is to emphasize the role of situational-contextual awareness, moment-by-moment, event-by-event, inch-by-inch, in creating the six aspects of self; that ancient humorous mystery of humanity.   I commend the reader to the joy of the concerted productive activity of creating opportunity (relating) and social value (sharing) with self, others, and Nature.

I like what I have accomplished with this beginning effort and I hope you benefit. Please give me your feedback and suggestions. This book is a "pebble" being tossed into the pond of human awareness. Who can say how far and how full the ripples may run?

What is relationship? What is this **self** which I've been told to seek? What, indeed? I've given a lot, a little, a great deal, and almost no (depending upon the period of my life) thought to these questions. My pursuit has given me an appreciation of the Buddhist proverb which tells us that living is a choice of action <u>and</u> direction. The proverb is: "To every person is given the key to the gates of heaven; the same key opens the gates to hell."

Today many people seek to have their lives <u>done</u>, as they have their hair <u>done</u>, or their taxes <u>done</u>, or their etceteras <u>done</u>.   This is not a "done" type book; this is a book about awareness and productive activity in living - a reminder to pay-attention-to and work-on living.   In the market place professional advice is for sale or lease, and in the community interpersonal and media advice is free or dirt cheap. Advice does not get your life <u>done</u>. You have to "<u>done</u>" your own life. Effort in living is a personal affair. Sweat-equity of spirit, as with sweat-equity of any self-aspect, has to be earned.

Living is not a game to be won or lost. Living is an art form expressed by each person in chosen, created degrees of cooperative socialness (moral living). There comes the moment to each of us when we know that we "will no longer live forever." The trigger for this flash to our reality can be as varied as there are people. Such events as a parent's or sibling's death, a note in a history book, or a deep personal illness may stir us to a new awareness. The University of Living's alma mater is a song of awareness, reality checks, and grace under pressure. Are we talking tournament golf here? Or, perhaps, the purple-hazed pleasure of angioplasty?

Given that life is terminal, how does a person create joy in living? Distress is bred through immature, irresponsible self-interest. Joy in living, on the other hand, results from combining work (active productivity) with self-knowledge and relationship. The feedback from relationship - Act #2 of that humorous mystery which we're all stumbling around darkly trying to unravel - tells us that the "psychological world" <u>does</u> exist and lies anchored between self and unself (others and Nature).... It is social, not selfish.

Much of what we call intelligence (aka IQ) is an expression of awareness; what we call genius is spasms of creativity based in a person's accrued pool of awareness. The former is a mirror of our experience in living; the latter, a blender-rendering which sums the parts into a fresh new whole of awareness.

Awareness is directed, informed action. Awareness involves past, present and future. Awareness is a human trait that can be improved with experience and time. Animals are alert. Humans are aware. Awareness is a full-context activity.

When one stands with his/her back to the Future, attention riveted on the Past, life, in passing, seems surprising, complex, uncontrollable... and, for some, painfully sad. Pleasure is rooted in mental, emotional, spiritual, and physical activity that occurs in the Present and is projected into the immediate and distant Future. Relationship that is created in productive activity, respect, patience, and humor moment-by-moment with others, self, and Nature is joy's sweet fountain of opportunity and value.

Opportunity, however, does not call out to you like a childhood friend who is passing your gate. Opportunity is a product of Activity. You create opportunity in your involvement with living.

Opportunity is in <u>your</u> next step. Opportunity is part of the dance. It's up to you to create a dance of joy, or desperation, boredom, or excitement. Context is an open forum.

Speaking of desperation - a fear of loneliness - consider how it influences us to associate with people with whom we hold but one common vibration: the wish to reduce our desperation. Desperate plus desperate equals, not double desperate... but desperate to the infinite power. This is when the Law of Human Bad Choices piles on the hot ashes. While the power of infinity edges toward big numbers, in this human relationship-event it equals nothing: tragic magic in the form of <u>A</u>bsolute <u>Z</u>ero.

Fear does not always jump out at you from the shadows and yell, "BOO!" At times fear is quite subtle. Just as you cannot sweep water into a pile, you can't do away with fear in the human adventure. Our fears are, however, clear tracks to self-knowledge. When we recognize our fears by using contextual awareness our fears can become an excellent teacher for reducing gridlocked, habitual thoughts and ineffective behaviors.

When Thales (about 2500 years ago) said that knowing self was most difficult, I sense that he spoke of a multi-aspect self. He may have determined aspects I have yet to experience. Nothing has changed, over the centuries, in this living adventure of social humans; still today knowledge of self scores high on the "grunt" scale. If you think human-to-human relating is in trouble, out-of-sync, destructive...take a peek at the sad situation existing between humans and Nature. Word on the street has it that Nature is filing for divorce. Context is, indeed, an open forum. Be aware! Chains are often required.

This book is about blending personal awareness and personal choices with social-ecological awareness and social-ecological choices. To step smartly on a living path of social cooperation, personality balance and harmony, morality, and sanity is every good soul's dream. Dance of the Pyramids is a pretty context in which 1) to pace-off this gossamer weave of will and wish, and 2) to refresh a personal motive of awareness and joy.

Relationship: Its X's and Its O's

Our inability to relate and share may be the misstep and stumble to our final downfall. Current global distress is not so much due to the increasing number of people on the planet as it is due to fatal non-relationship creating. The pyramids ain't dancin'! The hard part of life is found in living it, moment-to-moment; but the fun part of life is found also in the moment-to-moment living. Life's best moments, our honored, historic mentors tell us, are found in her stiffest challenges. Why would they lie? Our experiences and emotional awareness, our responsible maturity tell us that social is better than loneliness; love, better than fear; altruism, better than greed.

What makes up relationship? Can I grasp it, hold it in my hand? Are the links of this chain more air than steel? Relationship is a process, not a circumstance. It is created, not found. Time-space coupling is not relationship. Two people together do not a relationship make by their mere spatial togetherness. Skins touching is not the same as selves touching.

Life is a journey of choices, an ever changing process, an adventure of learning. Learning social cooperation is the key to pacing your life effectively with Nature, others, and self. All acts of living, both personal and interpersonal, are based upon contextual choices, concepts and theories. A Personal Philosophy of Life forms the primary stones at each level of each person's Pyramid of Wisdom.

What answer comes to mind when you ask yourself: "How do I view the world? It is an okay place? A troubled place, but capable of improving? A hopeless hell-hole? What are my assumptions about living?" Your answer tells you much about you. In living, your assumptions are <u>created</u> relative to how you evaluate changes and choice points of moment-by-moment events and thoughts. The color of your future is a personal designation. Assumptions and expectations are twins, birthed by beliefs and sired by attitudes, conceived in the beds of our past joys and disappointments.

Soren Kierkegaard told us, "Life can only be understood backwards; but it must be lived forwards." And Carl Jung said, "If you feel that the problems of life have been all solved, then something important has been lost."

Life, it seems, is destined to be confusing and uncertain - no matter how we search for predictors, astrological lodestars, inductive research, or advice. No one has been able to turn life around on its axis, as it were. Answers to living can be found only in hindsight, when the event is behind us. Answers are not pre-formed as so many puzzle parts to be placed in a pattern of total predictability. This is because at birth memory is an empty bucket and your experiential tote-sheet shows mostly zeros and blanks. To change this fact of birth would be to tamper with Nature...and God only knows what new ills we might produce in doing so.

Some people view life as an expanding circle, a rolling wheel, with each experience coming back for review and analysis; and others see life as a straight time-line, a linear march into infinity. It is said that time can be viewed as both vertical and horizontal... or as either, alone. Say what? Is this a special mind-screw-moment dance? Vertical time?

Life is a process of moment-to-moment decision making based upon continuous information. The more aware one is of his/her contextual interactions with Nature, self, and others the more accurate is the information and the more reliable the process of decision making.

Awareness is knowledge with action. It is not merely being informed. Awareness always entails creative involvement. Context is ever changing, for change is part of context.

To live well is to create special moments... not hours, not days, not weeks, not years, but moments. Only God can lay claim to feats of greater duration. To create special moments interacting with Nature, self or others is to live well. Be pleased to share in the moment. Do not despair in clutching for God's crown by wishing for enduring miracles. Leave the things of God to God. Take each moment... and do it well. You'll find it's all you can manage and you'll find that it is enough. Whoops, context just birthed a change,.. and another... and... whoops, there goes the last rubber tree plant.

Augustine said that God creates the universe new every day. Each day, each moment to the contextually aware person is a new delight in living. We, in our consumptive-based approach to life, have lost this inspiring aspect of living. We plod rather than dance, we curse rather than sing, we spectate rather than participate. We do not encounter self and others as curious, new, and fresh, but as fearful, stale, and boring. Most people have such a set role, that, I have to admit, it is difficult to see any variance from year to year much less moment-to-moment. Do not cut yourself off from change, from the natural flow and rhythm

11

of life. We are of seasonal Nature, of the active self, and of the social hum. Life is moving and changing, flow with it and affirm your quest constantly. Do not try to own the flowers of life. Enjoy them in their season, place and time. Do not kill the flowers so that you can carry a dying blossom to your home. This is to say: be involved in life where it is happening; do not alter it artificially and in a self-interested way. As we leave a flower for others to pleasure in, so we should leave the earth... at least as well as we found it. Much of our unhappiness comes from our awareness that we rape Nature (we destroy ourselves in this). With fear as our tutor we plunder. We pollute, we destroy the planet. Our nest is being rent by the poly-polar winds of ignorance and self-interested mischief. We are killing our species, and instinctually each person knows this. Do <u>not</u> play it again, Sam... but rather create the new and the fresh. Drink freely from the well of will and wishes, holding wisdom, not fear, to be your cup and your companion. Will it be <u>homo destructivus</u> or <u>homo sapiens</u>? Your choice! My choice! Our choice!

When it comes to facing the risk inherent in creating a relationship, a couple of old frontier sayings fit for me: 1) "The cowards never started, and the weak died along the way." and 2) "If you can't find the circumstances you want in life, create them!"

> "He who knows nothing, loves nothing. He who can do nothing, understands nothing. He who understands nothing is worthless. But he who understands also loves, notices, sees... the more knowledge is inherent in a thing, the greater the love... anyone who imagines that all fruits ripen at the same time as the strawberries knows nothing about grapes."
>
> Paracelsus

Words are frequently our worst detour away from understanding. Each person uses words in a personal way and reads from a particular point of view. Often even the writer does not understand the words so boldly used, so freely tossed at the page, so subjectively overlapped. Who is this Paracelsus anyway? And what is a Mike Nally? Whose words are on these pages, the writer's or the reader's? Who <u>are</u> you?

Many people seek relationship for much the same reason a soldier hurries to dig a foxhole... to be safe from the injuries of the passing events in the environment. But for most of us "relationship foxholes" too soon become a deep pit from which we can not easily emerge. At some point the shadow of boredom brings its chill to our hide-out. In our "secure" ruts we find meaning in the words "Safe but sorry"; a sense of loneliness leads us to blame life... and to become pessimistic in our daily outlook. Could this be a hint as to why not <u>all</u> caged birds sing?

Indeed, what if, as Virgil, Horace, et al., thought, "life is a perpetual cycle and aimless repetition of identical events" and "all our progress is an imprisonment in methods, but not in purpose"? Is it, perhaps, true that "there is nothing new under the sun; all is vanity and a chasing after the wind"? Such ideas are seeds for pessimism, and difficult to dismiss when one keeps a running tally in life's ledger.

The search for stress management techniques and dodges is <u>BIG</u> today - to name a few: relaxation, busyness, activities, drugs, cigarettes, coffee, newspaper reading, T.V., music, shopping, buying things, spending money, sex, shrinks (big and little, male and female, hetro-, homo-, and bisexual), born-again religion, war, and a nervous hum. While we sense that relationship is a hot clue for a safe exit from stress's maze, many of us prefer to embrace mythical "quick" solutions that demand a minimum of personal-social involvement. We keep the light dim in our rut, and we count on luck.

When we choose not to create balance and harmony with Nature, self, and others, we permit the foul-breathed, snarling, fanged dogs of distress to corner us. Yet, we ignore Nature, are confused by self, and our bond with others is often toilet-tissue thin. How far away can stress be? Is stress the next name on your dance card? One! Two! Cha-cha-cha! Aauugh!

As a social animal, we humans find loneliness to be our most stress-ridden event. But loneliness is not a condition a person has. Loneliness is not an affliction of something. Loneliness is a State of Being: A vacuum-packed existence devoid of relationship. Relationship with Nature, self, or others results only from the combined <u>aware effect</u> of relating and sharing. Relationship <u>is</u> the dance of the pyramids.

Our educational system has burdened us with a false lead when we seek to create relationship. To think that relationship books contain absolute solutions or answers is to misstep. Relationship books only contain information. Information based upon past events from other people's experience-fields. This information is at times stimulating, but too often merely cutely clever. We all know, for example, that men do not come from Mars, nor do women come from Venus. Some just seem that way, regrettably. What we <u>really</u> want to create in living is a progressive personal and commutual balance and harmony here on Earth,.. as earthlings, FCOL. The personal gems of knowledge and wisdom have a much higher sweat-to-polish index than mere information-exposure. Experience shouts that cute cleverness brings a pale whit of enduring light to one's personal reality. Such fad trivia are detours, away from the creative dance floor of living, to the "spiked" punch bowl and dim backroom of distracted immaturity. You don't want to go there. Trivium, however cute, however sweet, is <u>never</u> enduring.

Context-relevant questions and answers, the code keys of information, are formulated in the mind of the individual. Information without inquiry and application does nothing. Far from being "power", passive information is but the

thin shadow of the dead past, and may better remain buried in the books, if no applied effort is made to contextually understand and experientially interpret it. R. G. Robinson said, "Access to information is required for power, but access by itself does not create power." To never put the wheels on the soap-box and run it down the slope, to never test it, is to deny a crate with a wind shield the chance to be a racing champion.

Experience-awareness, in the form of questions and answers, is within each of us. This is our personal source of the energy and light needed to transform information's hazy fog into lucid, bright activity. As Eugene Field told us: "All human joys are swift of wing, /For heaven doth so allot it, /That when you get an easy thing, /You find you haven't got it."

In these "modern" days, change comes so quickly that our entire method of living is lurching and lunging, and dry-heaving all over the dance floor. Our psychic constructs are gasping and our spiritual inner-eye is glazed. We have, for the greater part of the circle, accepted without applied inquiry the hand-me-down mores of our ancestors. Mores that did not, in many ways, work all that well for our elders even in their slower-moving, less-populated times.

Here on the eve of the 21st Century we are caught in the confusing rush of mobile, thickly populated, global living. We should be so evolved... but we are not. Times are changing too rapidly, from all directions, for willy-nilly, awareless social-styles and communal klutzing to be effective. Unexamined, out-dated, overlapping, borrowed mores go stale quicker than the cross-culture "fast food" leftovers we fill our refrigerators with daily. They won't work for us, nor will they work for our children. It is time for us to reshuffle the deck and cut the cards anew. It is time for us to learn about creating awareness, balance, harmony, and rhythm-setting in relationship with Nature, self, and others. Hi ho! Hi ho! It's off to play we go! Oh, and remember--you can't almost dance.

We humans have been more studied in the breeding of livestock and pets than in creating and charting effective, collective social-conduct. Some "experts" and assorted wags say that "we're dancin' in the dark." What is a reasonable personal-interaction-goal? I think 50% positive, 35% neutral, and 15% negative is manageable and acceptable. I call this my "85% goal". This goal permits for a 15% margin of mis-matches and failed dud-encounters. But it also encourages a daily effort at a rewarding degree of positive outcome. Currently, most of us live at a less-than-25% non-stress-fueled interactive-level. The currents of change have swept over us and left us tumbling battered in the wake. We need to gain the forward crest and surf the social tide's changing, charging force. Most often the scenario is: "The force is with you!".... Then zip!... "It ain't." A plunging, purging trip to the bottom, in surf-babble, is called "purling." It's rarely pretty, never pleasant. When you "purl," the wave rolls over you without so much as a "Kiss my grits, Buckaroo!"

Every person must, like Sisyphus, make the daily journey up life's hill. Some go farther than do others in their allotted time... only to have each newborn take up their turn at rolling that marvelously resistant Stone of Trials. Human history is an endless cycle of starting over; as one person reaches their point of greatest  advance, then come others, new generations, taking up a place at the bottom and starting up the hill burdened by their own personal stone. Are there any hints scribbled in the Sands of Time at the bottom of the hill guaranteeing that any of us will reach the hill's mythical summit... and that we'll stay there? Does experience help? <u>Aware</u> experience, yes.

This century's miracle, the expectancy of a longer life span in the more affluent global sectors, is far from being every newborn's legacy of grace. The social viruses of prejudice and poverty place too many babes in grim mangers unvisited by the Magi: Faith, Hope, and Charity. A global community of balance and harmony, comprising <u>all</u> the aspects of self, is the only means to rout the Four Horsemen of the Apocalypse and their gnarly kin. A world-<u>dis</u>order ruled by immature, impulse-driven appetites is in deep-sick trouble. Is it any wonder that <u>sui</u>-cide among our teenagers and young adults is moving up the chart? Will granny and gramps be next? How should a person, a community, a nation, a world spell relief? Should it be written **y-o-u-t-h**? Or should it be written **r-e-l-a-t-i-o-n-s-h-i-p**?

It has long been held in many cultures that youth is a dis-ease for which age is the cure. Yet, in this country we ardently seek the illness and shun the remedy. Youth has the energy to be an agent for change, but it lacks wisdom. Youth dances to an impatient beat. Awareness between achievement and character, between a weed and a flower, and between a productive activity and "15-minutes" of cheap fame is vital to balance and harmony. Self-interest is warping our societal/ecological "mind and motive" in favor of its own perpetuation. The human tragedy-traumas of the 20th Century have cast many of us into an Augean stable of existential gloom where despair and ignorance mug wisdom and hope.

Youth is not enough! High tech is not enough! Dumb luck is not enough! And certainly cute cleverness is not enough! Who's choreographing our current dance, anyway? It's a dance without a scent of the future. A dance we're all party to, woefully. A dance that Mother Nature hopes we humans will retire-- 'cause we're stomping serious "mudholes" in her and in her pal Pogo.

Can somebody stop us, or not? Can somebody stop me? Stop you? Can <u>we</u> save <u>us</u> from <u>ourselves</u>? Or are we too-far crazy? That special some-"body", Pogo suggested, has got to be <u>us</u>. Gad, does that mean that irresponsibility is out? We seem to believe: "I exist, therefore I am involved. I eat, therefore I know nutrition. I have sexual intercourse, therefore I love. I think others are to blame, therefore I am okay. I have--" Why are you looking at me like that? Is my frustration peeking through the frayed fabric of my patience... again?

The human-need to evolve and strive is well-said in the quote: "It is not that we have set our goals too high and failed to reach them. But that we have set our goals too low, and we have reached them." Tell me the obvious and I usually giggle,.. because the obvious makes me nervous. Our global educational mission for many generations to come is quite obvious. I'm giggling. Are you giggling? Pogo and his friends, by the way, spell relief the same way I do: r-e-l-a-t-i-o-n-s- h-i-p. I hope you join us in this creative Q & A group-minuet.

Was it General Sherman who said, "War is life"? Oh, no, I remember. One of my brothers wrote that to me in a letter. Sherman must be the one who said, "Forgive them, Father, for they don't have a clue." But, without any giggles, let me ask you: "Is life war?" Is it from this bleak singular framework, from this dark dungeon of fear which we shape our rules, laws, mores, philosophies, our quirks and whims? If life is war, then human relationship seems condemned to never exceed the base struggle of animal-level activity--one person pitted against another embroiled in a nightmare of selfish competition. But if life is <u>not</u> war, then we can dream of and strive for higher-level activities. We can dream of meeting people with whom we can relate, share, and create social cooperation. Good teams in sports are made-up of people who play well together in a cooperative flow with a common purpose. So, too, are good communities made up of people of comparative flow and common purpose. Like Bobby Kennedy said, "... I dream and ask why not."

We all have dreams, and we all try to understand, or perhaps some only take random guesses at, the social dance that will bring us together cooperatively with Nature, self, and others. The superstars, the volunteer behind the desk at the library, and the cute youngster all bundled-up waiting for the school bus on a cold winter's morning... we all have dreams. Is one person's dream exactly as another's dream? Is it, perhaps the same dream for all of us? Is it a dream of relationship with the world... the world of Nature, self, and others? This is what I believe it is, however strangely some bring it to the dance floor. A simple dream, the same dream every moment, reflects itself in our every thought, gesture, mood, and action. A dream that says, "Life does not have to be war."

If it is so simple, why is relationship so elusive, so difficult to realize? Why is the dance floor of human endeavors littered with the wreckage of failed attempts? The snags are the jagged barbs of fear and ignorance. Ignorance can be erased with learning and experience, but the barb of fear is Hydra-like, ever recurring. "Ignorance," it's been said," is not a curse, it's a choice." But fear is with us from the "git-go," and ever present... or coming at a gallop.

As fragile human infants we need the constant help of others from our first moment as we begin the natural struggle for life. We humans are motivated by fear; of which, we have fully as many strains as we have aspects of self. Just as physical fears are not allayed by fatigue or sickness, social fear can not be removed with inactive isolation. To practice that old saying: "Sometimes I sits and thinks, and sometimes I just sits" is to nurture the stressful bad health of paranoia. We fear the woods. We fear the streets. We fear isolation. We fear living. We fear dying. We fear that "something might be catchin' up."

Perhaps this book should be dedicated to loneliness. There certainly is a lot of it going around. But why? When at every turn and stile there's a person we have not yet come to know. Why, indeed. There are billions of people on this planet, and yet we speak of being lonely. How can that happen? Loneliness is a product of community vacuum. Without a collective personal effort to create opportunity and value the "zit" of isolating paranoia doth fester mightily. When paranoia blooms, potential and hope wilt. Fear makes victims of us all.

Indeed, high numbers of people do crowd and jam the human race, but density of bodies does not a community of harmony and balance make. "Alone in a crowd" is a common state in a mobile anomie. A herd has density. A flock has density. Are herds and flocks models of interactive, creative community? Wisdom's cup is seldom dipped, tipped, or sipped in such gatherings. In herds and flocks you just do herd and flock behavior.

When I sense that "Lonely" is entering my context, I like to believe that someone "special" is waiting for me, just ahead in the next context to be created. I prefer to dance with hope, rather than mope with despair. I prefer to prune my paranoia, and nourish the belief that the stranger ahead is there to welcome and hug me, not assault and mug me. But I try to keep my randy appetites and passions from running, crazy and naked, off the cliffs of RISK and DARE with my sometimes naive social curiosity. "Prudential" is not just an insurance company, it's, also, a great pace-ingredient. Gently stir it in.

Our current collective draft of modern day <u>Tales of Alice and Allan in Wonderland</u> are tales of woe. The pessimistic indexes measuring our relationships with Nature, others, and self say that we're in free-fall: we've gone over the edge. The optimistic voice tries to assure us by saying that all the data aren't in, yet. Let's focus our realities, lower our shields, and put away our barf bags in order that we may discuss, in earnest, why "cesspool" is displacing "cottage" as our favorite descriptive term of society. If we are to remedially determine the behavioral hazards and motivational detours that lead us to head-banging interactions and dream derailments, we need to fold away our addictions and denial. How, in this country, said to be the "richest and most powerful" in human history, can the dry-heaves of lost hope be happening to us? I guess, like the man said, "Life is trickier than it looks."

In recent decades we are discovering that our "genetic set of rules" are way different from our "social and ecological set of rules." Too often, too many of us strut and fret upon life's dance floor using single-switch motives and low-beam awareness. Our children, our messengers to the future, are scarred daily by our aware-less ignorance. Mostly, we adults don't even know which end of a prayer to take hold of, or why productive activity matters, or what an important role Hope plays in a strong community, personal well-being, nimble dance, or good cooking. What do we really have to teach our children about "poling a punt" through our present day Okefenokee of living? Ignorance of self is never bliss.

A popular detour into ignorance directs us to the belief that with over five billion people on this planet there is but one way to relate and share. Truth is: there is but one people on this planet, and billions of ways to create opportunity and value.

People are connected and drawn to each other by two primary forces, 1) by Nature, as are all organisms to their own kind, and 2) by the shared values created through the uniquely human-motive of social self. To deny the pre-eminent importance of shared social values is to deny the human part of personality.

To know that we, each and all, occupy the same passing time-frames can help us avoid panic's rush. When we join shoulders in pushing the stone of personal, ecological, and social responsibility up the mountain of life, then will we, taking heart in the witnessed efforts of others, resuscitate our crucified hope for balance and harmony in living. A response in the direction of community and global well-being, so rapid as to thrill one's spirit, is not only possible, it is damn-well likely.

Relationship has no plot. When a plot exists in a posture of sharing, it is deception, not sharing. Love does not, for example, have a target. Love is freedom from fear. It is not love that becomes disappointment, it is fear that knows disappointment. Let's turn the lights on. Let's be aware!

Awareness is vital to the healthy development of personal, social, and ecological character (aka pyramid building). Without awareness character pales, wilts, fails to thrive. Character suffocation is a furtive form of death. You may not always see physical signs of such suffocation, but often you can. Physical suffocation is, of course, the result of an absence of air. Character suffocation is the result of an absence of spirit. Both forms of suffocation are real and lethal. Character suffocation is a silent nightmare. No blood flowing from an open vein, just muted agony. To be without a resonating, respiring spirit is to be without Faith, without Charity, without Hope,.. without a tick, without a tock,.. without an eenie, a meenie, a miney, or even a moe. It's a way-deep "one-holer."

It's a gradual process this living:

> The road is long, take it one pebble at a time;
> The mountain is high, take it one step at a time;
> The ocean is wide, take it one wave at time;
> The life is short, take it one event at a time;
> The relationship is sweet, take it one
> moment at a time.

My niece, Dian Stanton Beary 11/17/80

It is the absence of spirit, of active character, of a broader awareness that brings many humans to be captive slaves of a selfish, narrow purpose in living. The only way we are permitted, as conspired, no doubt, by Mother Nature and God, to create living is one moment at a time. But it is not the only way we can perceive living. In our early years our motives are primarily appetite rooted. These fundamental urges are not exactly exemplar workshops in effective relationship. Many of us awarelessly become their prisoners and end-up career-dancing like wounded animals motivated by the limited passions of a lesser self. There is no "Zip-a-dee doo dah" in swill-dancing. My, how we struggle, agonize, hit foul balls, and collect scar tissue in our limp across life's dance floor.

Just as good coaches can shape winners into champions, and good teachers can encourage eager minds to be creative minds... so, too, can successful experience transform one's fear of risk into a stimulus for romancing challenge. It is not the event that is scary; it is our reluctance to create new responses that causes fear to bubble and rush-up in us. When we become threatened, by whatever name it's called, we become protective of self. And as parents we become protective of our children and family--our extended-self. Protectionism begets paranoia; paranoia begets isolationism; isolationism results in fenced-in loneliness. When we build a "paranoid pyramid" the idea of close dancing to honor the full context of living becomes a "slim-to-none" option. The bedrock of fun is to offer new responses to old cues, when appropriate, and creative responses to unique stimuli, when context permits. Fun dwells in dancing with challenge.

As biologically themed organisms, we humans live one breath, one pulse beat, one intervening variable, one appetitive moment at a time. However, we are better served, as aware-potential memory banks, to evaluate our life motives, purposes, pathways, and strategies using a savory blend of past, present, and future. It is within this extended context-awareness that balance in tactics, style, goals, and objectives may occur, and where personal rhythm may be created. To best see the valley, a climb, now and then, to the mountain top is recommended.

Recurring casualties in living are those people who allow the moment to be of greater or of lesser weight and duration than it is due. To avoid this web-site of disappointment, grasp the moment, but do not become its hostage; use the full, extended context of living as your relative-index of living effectiveness. Create a living path of productive activity, patience, respect, and humor. Let your bouquet for the dance be colored and shaped by self-aspect exercises, active practice, evaluated experience, and a smart-awareness of relationship with Nature, self, and others. Mr. Shakespeare had Enobarbus tell Lepidus, in Act II, Scene II of <u>Antony and Cleopatra</u>, "Every time serves for the matter that is then born in't." I agree, if this says what I think it says. However, with Mr. "S" I'm never quite certain. Like a fellow once said, "Don't believe everything you hear, even when you're talking to yourself."

Hung-over, honky-tonk "one-night stands," in whatever deceptive mask, are not where relationship comes to be born or conceived. Relationship has <u>nothing</u> in common, kin, or kind, with "appetite abuses," nor is it deserving of the crass messages found scribbled on bathroom walls and toilet stalls. It is not the nature of relationship that is at fault, but rather it is our begging awareless-ness that brings the dream of relationship to be a yoke on our spirits, and an anvil on our minds. Do you believe that relationship is an impossible myth, God's worst punishment passed-on to us through Adam and Eve (Did they do <u>anything</u> right?)? Do our war chronicles and divorce-court files accurately witness that human passions are but a deceiving, destructive "nub" of blind self-interest, and that hope of enduring relationship is Tantalus's "Frumious Bandersnatch"? Is social stress, that self-induced emotional and spiritual lobotomy, the only dance partner available? As our collective Karma puckers sour, is loneliness the conceded victor over social-self? Are we talking "impossible"? Where's our Sense of Humor, FCOL?

Relating and sharing are our most important social resources. And humor is our key means of dealing with the Impossible. Humor is that unique human fuel for striving, creating, working, and enduring when under challenge's burden. All conflicts in living, from the mere to the impossible, result from snags to head-on collusions between, or among, self, others, and Nature. "Fun" in living is created by greeting challenge and accepting its offer to dance. To respect challenge's nod is to feel your spirit smile. When your Sense of Humor pales, wilts, fades, or retreats your creative Sense of Well-being staggers and "head-plants" into the ditch of distress. A person's Sense of Humor is a direct offspring of that person's level of relating and sharing. Humor is born in relationship, and it is nourished by awareness.

Relating to self, Nature, and others is the entry-way to the social trove of wealth, health, and happiness. Sharing with others and Nature is our source of balance, harmony, peace, and joy. And productive activity, respect, patience, and humor are the eenie, the meenie, the miney, and the moe of the living ingredients for the creation of the good life,.. of social/ecological cooperation. Not even Baking Soda can claim more.

These past several decades have beat the drum loudly and "oftenly" that "profits and profligacy make our society bulletproof," and our current cultural mantra of "We be cool! We be cool! We be VERY cool!" praises personal excess as superior to personal balance. We've rushed to accept the seductive invitation to splash and frolic in rude appetite, while our dreams for living well in social cooperation, assassinated by our excessive indulgence, are strewn like so many rotting fish on the paranoid beaches of our frantic passage. Yeah, we be <u>REAL</u> cool. This "Beach Party" is being run by aware-less "slaves of profit," and we honor them with our aware-less attendance. We be <u>SUPER</u> cool. Are we, indeed, having fun, yet? Is there one single relationship carcass that is not nailed to the stenchy, fecal-steeped floor of our modern-day Augean stables? Does anyone have Hercules's 911 number? "This is Dogpatch calling Hercules! Come in, pooh-leeeze. We be so cool, we be freezin'."

(Writer's aside)

While the band takes a short "break," let's chase the chill of loneliness by gathering in the warmth of friendship. Let's pull up a stump, kick off our dancin' shoes, and take a "few" to stir some "bonded" summary thoughts into our cups of refreshing, imaginary punch. Ah,.. I <u>be</u> comfortable,.. how you <u>be</u>?

<u>Some "kick-back" moments</u>:

The three jewels in the crown of relationship are self, Nature and others. To create, from moment-to-moment, harmony and balance between these precious concepts is to experience (in looking back at our living) a life time of great good and happiness. A Greek adage says, "Life is the gift of Nature, but beautiful living is the gift of Wisdom." A <u>good</u> society comes from sharing our created social and ecological value with Nature and with others. To abuse self, others, or Nature is to abuse the potential good in life.

Mr. Aldus Huxley (in his <u>Texts and Pretexts</u>, p. 129) told us, "Living is an art; and, to practice it well, men need, not only acquired skill, but also a native tact and taste." Mr. Huxley then added, "We are all poets of living - for the most part, alas, pretty bad poets."

Did you read Huxley's words with thoughtful consideration or with speed-reading haste? What do <u>you</u> take from his comment that we need "... native tact and taste"? Are you creating this book, or just reading it? How's your Awareness Alarm working?

This is <u>NOT</u> a "how-to" book. Here, we are exploring Society, not Civilization; Living, not History; Created Process, not Pre-set Predictability; Art, not Science. The silent print on these pages is here to encourage mutual self-discovery and creative personal-growth. These muted words are not offered merely to serve as more fodder for some back-alley dumpster or to add "memory-bank" litter to our fly-infested, historic landfills of "permanent" discards.

It is Civilization and Law that are the external attempts at making living permanent: Things to be learned and memorized. A Civilization and its Laws can collapse and vanish. Society, in converse, is a process, a moving current of which we are, each and all, animate and important contributors. Society will be created so long as humans and Nature co-exist. We are all, in our sum, society; we are all social and ecological. We all know How society works, for we do the dance every moment... either with self, Nature, or others. Our society, at any given moment, reflects how well or poorly we collectively perform. How're we doing? You will not be reading in this book about things or ideas that you do not already innately know. It's our personal awareness that occupies a priority on my agenda. Remember: this is a book about Awareness, not about Advice. This is my book, your book,.. our book. This is our mutual creation in its "birthin'." Just as our society is.

Relationship is not a particular act or event that occurs alone in isolation. As a flower is not a petal, or a stamen, or a single leaf - it is a concept of total effect - so, too, is relationship a concept of total effect. Relationship is the sum effect of all our physical, mental, spiritual, and emotional events; relationship results from all of our self aspects' involvements, thoughts, and moods... blended in the ever-changing context of living.

Relationship is what we, each of us, create in living socially, ecologically, and personally with relative degrees of balance and harmony. It reflects us, it reflects our character, and our values. Relationship cannot be known by separating it into parts. Relationship is the total effect of the human act of creating society, which occurs one moment at a time. Society is what we do; relationship is us doing: us creating opportunity and us creating value.

Human living has meaning only in relationship. We have so much loneliness and so little social purpose in living today because we lack person-to-person, and person-to-Nature sharing. Human history tells us: Value is Power. Yet from behind drawn heavy drapes of paranoia, peek fear-filled mavens who describe the altar of power as the having of personal control over others or over Nature. The mono-theme of acquisition without character-development/achievement without value-creation sets our feet on a one-step anti-social dance of empty consumption. This is a minted path to social cul-de-dead-endedness. No sharing equals zero power.

The true coin of social and personal power is, in fact, relationship. Just as poetry is the expressed music of self, so, too, is sharing the empowerment of self. Only fear sees power as separate from relating and sharing; love never holds such a lonely view. It is not within relationship to do away with power; as relationship flourishes power is enhanced. The cooperative behavior of relationship provides a clear "profile in awareness" of power. The second face in the mirror, with relationship, is that of social and personal power. To "own" property or others is not power. To kill others or Nature is not power.... And, certainly, to kill self is not power. To create relationship, that is power. The butt-naked "poetry of wisdom" dwells in the understanding that the power of cooperative society, of moral ethics, as created through our individually unique, but collective, styles of relating and sharing is the strength of any nation. The concerted act of societal power, polished with balance and harmony, is expressed, moment-by-moment, through the human behaviors of productive activity, respect, patience, and humor. A strong society is hatched by an empowered people. A society's relationship-health reflects the collective self-health of its creators... you and me, and all the other Pogos and Dorothys. I hope we're not too "sheepled-up" by fear to recognize that we can't buy power, not with cash, not with plastic-credit. Power is not a "mall" item. Or as William Wordsworth sang, "Getting and spending, we lay waste our powers:..."

Regrettably, for all of us, many people have become deeply lost in their aware-less search for power over self, others, and Nature. Their daily paths lead, as in some dark fairy tale, into a howling woods of fear, loneliness, and pollution. In my youth, the resident intellectual at the local ACME pool hall, Louie the Rack shared his disappointment with me about his daily findings: "In seeking the pulse of life, my young fellow, I have often feared that I was fondling the wrist of a long-dead cadaver." (Louie did a great W.C. Fields imitation.) Perhaps, Louie searched in the wrong dumpsters. How's your search going? The key rule in "dumpster diving" is: "Don't let the heavy lid fall on your body parts."

As humans we hunger for the purpose of spirit. As animals we settle, too often, for the motive of mind. Since the Eden days of Adam and Eve to the primer play of Dick and Jane, establishing a balance between these surging aspects of self has been the theme of all human comedy and tragedy. Human history is the story of our "pushing a large stone up a steep hill." It is the story of "brain and body's" resolute resistance to our recalibrating self's inertial-motive system as championed by our "heart and soul." We humans, on average, seem only somewhat better evolved spiritually than a mushroom rooted in a rotting log in the Okefenokee swamp. The many who, today, hear Despair's loud message from the numerous killing fields and violent streets of the 20th Century--the message that screams, "It's beyond help!"--claim to be, at best, victims of a massive "Gotcha!" joke by a cruel God. "God who?" is a frequent question. Others say, "God is dead!" Yet, even a brief glance at the "ordered-chaos" of the Universe, a quick scan of the miracle of the human body, or at life's mystery itself, causes me to ask, "What the heck is all this? What is this infinite secret sensed deep within my-self that I hunger for?" In his own personal search, Tolstoy concluded, "Faith is the sense of life, that sense by virtue of which man does not destroy himself, but continues to live on. It is the force whereby we live." Faith is the force of spirit, it is not a measurable function of the mind.... And it is essential to aware, enriched living. At "Headbanger" moments, such as this, when I become envious of all life forms without a central nervous system, I recall Tennyson's lines of simple comparison:

> "Flower in the crannied wall,
> I pluck you out of the crannies,
> I hold you here, root and all, in my hand,
> Little Flower--but if I could understand
> What you are, root and all, and all in all,
> I should know what God and man is."

In choosing a course of behavior, too often, we look at only the <u>beginning</u>... resulting in our being amazed with the middle, and disappointed with the end. Immaturity, ignorance, a lack of awareness, and a shortage of foresight are far from blissful. They are the key ingredients most often used in Grief Pie:.. common fare in the market place of our daily dealings.

At this point, may I offer you some kicking-stones for the pathway of your thoughts? Ah, the band is back!

Getting into a rut is easy - it's all down hill.

The deeper you dig your rut, the darker living becomes. Despair is not having a tall enough ladder.

"We act as if living is tougher than trying to swallow a mouth full of fish hooks." (Attributed to Harvey Xu, the Mad Hatter's cousin.)

Relationship is given a boost by maturity and our respect for responsibility. Responsibility is not a barrier to freedom, rather it is a doorway to new horizons. The freedom to choose, to participate, to create new horizons carries the duty of our being Responsible and Mature.

In living well, it is not a matter of <u>rising to the occasion</u>, it is a matter of <u>creating the moment.</u>

"My journey is more important to me than any goal." The quote was said to me by my sister Joan Robinson, a long time dancing partner of mine. What could she have meant?

Living well is an active event, not easily done by the oxy-moronic. Some people would like to believe that all they need in order to live well is to pose attractive and cut cute... and "it" will happen for them. Outcome? Disappointment. "Pin-ups" tend to fade in the contextual stretch... of a life-time.

A person who depends upon the "preparation of others" is a <u>user</u>. No planning, no attention to details, no preparation, no awareness leads to user-ism.

The motto of a user: Free is better than cheap.

Beware: Users and slobs do not readily alter their droppings.

The "How to" books that talk about building a table tell us to take wood, nails, hammer, saw, etc.,.. to <u>buy these</u> at the store. It doesn't work that way in the "What to" world of living. In the "What to" of living, the needed materials are attitude, values, awareness, respect, trust, etc. These "things" can not be <u>bought</u>. We have to forge these living tools over time, and create their image from our experience bank.

It is up to each of us to create our Path in Living. No one follows an already set way - since each of us is unique, such set ways do not exist. No matter how hard a parent tries to control a child's destiny, or a child tries to march the course of a parent - living does not clone in all of its sundry phases and aspects. Context can be "Hell--served--for--breakfast," at times. But "Choice, not chance, determines the course of one's path," said an unknown warrior of living-motivation.

Adversity is not a mountain to be overcome. Adversity is, at best, an <u>excuse</u> for giving up in Life's Journey. Adversity is a natural part of the journey.

An ancient sage, the local drunk in my boyhood hometown, advised: "Do not think that you know the world." He was "looped" but lucid in serving his curb-side ministry. There is always a corner, a niche, to be lived and learned, a new dance to be created. O.W. Holmes taught, "The greatest thing in this world is not so much where we are, but in which direction we are moving."

In life's journey the primary load points in relating with self, others, and Nature are Joining and Separating. For example, the birth of a child is a Joining, while death of a loved one is the starkest form of Separating; knowledge of self is a joining, while self-deception is a separating event. How would you choose to define "pyramid dancing?" Whom would you invite? It's your choice. It's your party. Are eenie, meenie, miney, and moe on your guest list?

Regrettably, the "Hug and Love" model of current Educational Philosophy is too often only cosmetic or surface. The model is akin to dusting-off a pitched and battered bronco rider, giving a smile, a pat on his/her bruised ass, but not telling him/her anything useful about what to do to stay on the horse.

Humans used to worry about how to avoid dying, now we worry about the <u>burden of survival</u>, such as boredom, sex after sixty (or seventy or eighty), not making a fool of ourselves in a marathon before <u>all</u> those witnesses. No matter how we turn it, flip it, or palm it...we assume that everything comes up "tails."

Have our addictions taken the place of relationship in our living process? It seems that we try to defy the laws of emotional gravity and the limits of schizophrenia by seeking to be <u>happy</u> and <u>sad,</u> <u>anxious</u> and <u>relaxed</u> at the same time. "We're stressed in more directions than a pigmy's condom on King Kong!" a toilet-stall wag in Leesburg, Virginia would advise us. Let's check our daily roster of distractions: nicotine, caffeine, alcohol, aspirin, narcotics, etc., sex, exercise, eating, spending, shopping, driving, music, leisure, travel, sports, TV, religion, information, work, money, speed, sleeping, computers, movies, the occult, school, soap operas, game shows, trivia, clichés. The list goes on and on. Any one of these "addictions" may not be hurtful to the body, but they all are, when done in excess, harmful to the spirit.

There is nothing else to the social human, but relationship. Is that hard to believe? Put the book down, go for a walk, relax, and think about it. What is society, but relationship? When relating and sharing are missing we have moved into something that is not social. It is too often suggestive of a jungle... a jungle filled with Fear, Loneliness, and Pollution. A true test of Humor: hung between the horns of a giggle and a scream.

I have heard it said, "We're defined by the relationships we create." I like it. But as my buddy Doctor Zero noted, "Am I really that bad?" How are your horizons looking? Are you keeping the litter picked up in your small corner of the Garden of Paradise? Clouds mottle everyone's patch of sky, at one time or another. How's the patch you were put in charge of? Sewn into the hem of Mother Nature's gown is this truism: "Trials are the nature of living. Horizons do not exist upon which a storm will never break." The horizon of your today is not the same horizon as of your yesterday, nor of your tomorrow. Even the calmest hut, one nested in the most tranquil of mountain meadows, can have its bolts split by a sudden earthly shrug. But many a wise man has said, "Man is best when in danger." If this is true, we humans are rapidly moving toward our grandest era.

Ah, ha! Isn't that br'er Pogo over there in a corner of the dance hall... beating the mucus out of himself? Could it be that he has met the enemy... and it is HIM, FCOL? Is it possible that the rest of us are "off the hook?" Why do I sense a "chronic chill" at this self-deceptive notion of elation over victimizing others? "Hit your-self once for me, Pogo!"

Is that the patter of Hypocrisy's "tiny" feet that I hear? My sarcasm runs away with my awareness, when ever I consider joining a consortium of pixy-led profiteers and promoters. "Hang in there, Pogo! I think your match is about to get top-billing." My self-interest acts against me, when it stirs my apathy: surely my most damning addictive-deception. To encourage our paling community to seek nourishment by sucking the bile of greed is not unlike giving a sickly child a "gin and tonic," instead of applesauce and tapioca. Our fears are "conning" us.

For example, can we continue to allow the "money stackers" to pontificate, in the interest of profits, that Nature is a consumer item? Must our natural heritage, of dancing in freedom and joy with Nature, be available to us only for a fee? Is Mother Nature merely a purchasable "whore" held hostage from us behind coin operated turn-stiles by backroom hucksters and bureaucratic pimps? Will somebody STOP ME! Please? I feel a major case of "road rage" coming on.... Make that "book rage."

Oh, how readily a soaring attitude of goodwill and community can plunge and spiral under the burden of self-interested actions. Without harmony and balance in living it is difficult to create joy. Too quickly, it seems, can the dark clouds of personal insecurity's pettiness cover the face of community's moon; leaving no beginning, no middle, no end,.. no yesterday, no today, no tomorrow,.. no past, no present, no future,.. no faith, no charity, no hope,.. no lingering, no love, no longing,.. no poetry, no prose, no rhyme.... I really don't want to live like that.

Who is sent to know how human context will flow and eddy? It certainly will not be me. However, rumor, if we decide to honor it, holds that the historic "droppings" of our global contextual theme between cultures, races, religions and chefs, butlers and upstair's-maids has been one of endless discord, strife, and selfishness. Ah, human vanity... how grand your chaos, how bleating your gossip, how silly your strategy.

The cool night air and the veiling shadows near the garden's gazebo call to me: "Come!" Would you dance with me, as my attitude seeks to re-create its eager optimism and elevation? My memory doesn't want to be alone, right now. Dancing in the dark... alone... is not always what is best for one's "Gesundheit." In ten years, I wonder, what will our memories tell us of our current choices in creating our paths into a new century? Do we have even a glint of social cooperation,.. and ecological awareness? Or are we putting all our remaining energies straining "to hear the washer women gossip over the back fence"?

Human memory, our trace to the past, much like the tracks of a desert coyote chasing a terrified jackrabbit across a mud flat, can be altered by the stress of time (and vanity). Memory is where the footprints of our individually created yesterdays take refuse. It is in memory that we store the cool winds and gentle rain spent with friends of old, and, likewise, we store the thunder and lighting of the fearsome howling storms we've visited. What will our memories tell us of our choices made this day, this moment--balance and harmony or vanity and selfishness? Come on, Attitude! Climb, baby, climb!

When you, should you live so long, become the oldest person remaining with memories of your past,.. when your footprints alone mark the path from your yesterdays into your today,.. when you have, without impugnment and without debate, license to review your life's path from either the highroad of balance and harmony or from the low road of vanity... what, do you suppose, will Honesty suggest to you?

I note, without hesitation or reservation, that my fondest memories were created in social moments of special sharing: Etchings rendered in the tones and frame of social and ecological cooperation, awareness, respect, productive activity, patience, and humor... as embellished by Mother Nature's genius.

May I ask you: Of all the people you have known for, let's say, a year at least, in your life-time, how many do you have a "relationship" with today? Our mobile society certainly, even with near-kin, works against much of a lofty rating on the old 1-10 scale for most of us. Then we also encounter the bias: that

Youth creates opportunity much better than it creates value--relating is far more facile than is sharing in our "greening years." And for most of us, it's during our youth that we splash in the main currents of the population flow, of the discoveries, and of the games of living. Since relationship-creating is not an art-form of age, so much as it is of maturity, many of us beach, bottom-out, or hit-the-rocks early because our motivational "game plan" remains an immature trickle, "narrowed down to some one simple emotion or sensation of the body." (William James told me so.)

Relating and sharing, a couple of the key players in the X's and O's of creating relationship, find motive in each and every aspect of self. However, the continuous blending of changing context with the overlap and intermingling of the mental, the physical, the emotional, the spiritual, the social, and the ecological self-aspects can definitely blur the "blips" of motive on our screen of understanding. Without keen awareness, fear's disharmony and imbalance darkly shadows the sun, the moon, and the stars of our creative purpose. When at a loss for conceptual clarity, narrow bias of motive and behavior can "seem like a good idea at the time." Those people whose living is narrowly motivated by "one simple emotion or sensation of the body" most often are the one's who admire "hindsight" as being 20/20. Such aware-less people view paranoia as necessary and adaptive to survival... and they nurse an attitude so mottled by fear and insecurity as to make Joe Stalin and Edgar Allan Poe dance like a couple of cock-a-hooped, happy-go-lucky optimists. Have you sent your congress-person a "get well" card lately?

Relationship is, to be sure, elusive; possibly because we, in our laziness, and impulsive haste after convenience, want relationship to result from magic and dumb luck. Relationship's X's and O's are not responsive to the "remote" directives and whims of indolent selfishness. The beginnings of interpersonal relating occur when an individual moves beyond one's self with social feelings extended toward others. When this extension is respected and shared by others, these mutual "good" feelings blend in the productive activity of created community. When Nature is invited to participate equally in this living dance therein dwells the contextual-potential of balance, harmony, joy, and peace,.. known also as LOVE.

At this moment my step is sure, my pyramid is fit and tetrahedrally perky, and my attitude soars where only eagles dare. I be liking it. I hope you are doing as well.

Sharing = Creating Value with Others and Nature

"The deepest need in man is the need to overcome his separateness, to leave the person of his aloneness." In telling us this, Erich Fromm also suggested a strong dose of permanent "mature love" as the condition for satisfying this need. I can go for that idea. But it sounds like a mansion in the sky type thing. It's like saying: the answer to poverty is being rich. We all agree, but how do we get there from here?

The punch line, as Fromm told us, is mature love; the way to get there, I believe, is the productive activity of sharing. This sharing is something you do, it's not something you are. It is something you create (with others and Nature), it's not something you have. Sharing is a productive activity, a process: it's not an outcome or a condition of being. Sharing is not the mansion in the sky. Sharing is the pathway to that mansion. Sharing is a path with a heart: sharing is social and ecological. Anyone, of any age, can do this sharing, but you have to have others or Nature mutually involved in the act. "Partners in creating value," you might say. It's done together.

A young boy, whom I knew, once asked his dad, "Does a person need help to share?" His dad, who was a pretty thoughtful guy, replied, "Let me put it this way: when you try to clap with one hand, it's no longer clapping - it's called waving; or when you have sex with yourself, it's not sex - it's called masturbation. You know about that, right? And to share only with yourself is not sharing - it's called selfishness. Yes, son, to share, a person needs help." And in all my days since then, I've yet to hear an argument of any weight that convinces me that selfishness isn't lonely.

To share is not fiction. It is not an impossible dream. To share is a productive activity that involves self, others and Nature. Sharing doesn't come as a twilight gift from the Tooth Fairy, nor with age, nor by throwing rocks at an old abandoned house. Nor can it be bought in the market. Sharing has to be created moment-by-moment between self and unself. Unself, of course, is just another way to say others and Nature. Such word-alternates help me follow Ms. Gertie Gatens's advice. As my fourth grade teacher in St. Albans, W. Va.'s Central School she coached us young writers, "Try not to repeat yourself too often, even if you do want to fill in the page." Ms. Gatens has passed beyond giving shared advice. She died recently at 88.

Sharing is created inch-by-inch, day-by-day, joy-by-joy. You don't get sharing. You don't get shared on, shared to, or shared at. Anyone can seek to create sharing, but the snag is: sharing must be created mutually with others or with Nature. Just like the tango, it takes two to do this sharing dance. The creation of social and ecological harmony and balance between self, others and Nature gives rise to a peace-filled context of joy in living. No matter how tough,

mean or indifferent Nature and others may be at times, the potential for created sharing is the enduring rib of hope in human context. Take away sharing, and our fading hope leaves every dance to fear.

A foul-breathed contradiction to our social nature is loneliness. Resulting from a fear of others, a fear of Nature, and a deep lack of self-trust, loneliness is one of the "Three Black Ravens of Despair." Its job is to ambush all hopes a person holds for sharing. For those of us who concede sharing, in order to rush in "herded isolation" with the "madding crowd" in consumptive strife, find that we camp lonely, we hike lonely, we cook lonely.... We stay lonely even when squeezed into a crowded elevator. How is it possible to be lonely in a crowd: squeezed, circular, or other-sized? How many makes, shapes and models of personal dis-ease are there? Do I let my fears dictate my style and manner of daily dance? Do I aggressively take from others and Nature, or do I actively and awarely seek to create value (share) with the "unself" portions and factors of my context? Where does dis-ease end... and well-being begin?

A common comment about human choice is: "We're born knowing how to take. We have to learn to give." Taking is considered a natural, physically driven step in our dance of survival. While sharing, the art of giving <u>and</u> receiving, is to choose a social-cooperative "twist and turn." The cackling voice of fear, however, is present in both choices. "Without choice," it has been said, "there can be no freedom." A good, but limited notion, for, certainly, the mere presence of choice alone does not guarantee freedom. Our fears are laced with choices and our choices are marbled with fear. Did Dr. Doolittle confide that all the animals, by the way, even have a concept of "free"? They most certainly experience degrees of choice and the pulse of fear. Animals of higher cortical development seem, as well, to experience loneliness. But I have yet to find any hint that aside from humans (and seemingly far too few of us) there resides any "food-chain" concern with pollution (Black Raven #3). Fear is self-based, loneliness is other-determined, and pollution is Natures-related in human-awareness terms. The twisted course of human existence is not simple by a loud shout. A single person, e.g., can be relatively "free", for a moment, of the crashing waves of fear and pollution,.. but still be dismally lonely. Why?

Because sharing, the antidote for loneliness, is a mutual creation. The fear that dwells in the context of others often acts to exclude a person... and mutuality dies. It saddens me to see others turn away in harbored strife from friends and family. Such an assassination of the past provides a ripe compost for the "kudzu of loneliness" to fully spread and choke the garden of your living beauty--and it closes me out of your future. A lose-lose event. (By the way, do birds-of-the-wild <u>know</u> they are "free"? or even care? Or do they only know that they are "hungry," e.g.?)

A few weeks ago I had a chat with a 22 year old fellow who had dropped out: out of college, out of energy, out of knowing what to do next. He had a Ferris Wheel type manner without the amusement park flavor of a good time. I would call him a dulling manic-depressive. At one point (near the bottom of a rotation), he said, "I don't try to meet new people anymore. I'm too paranoid. They're too paranoid. Swapping fear is not fun after a while. I watch the darting eyes and frowning faces drift around me. I'm sure this is what being crazy feels like. It's totally weird. People all over the place, and I'm alone. I hate it!" I told him I thought anybody would hate it. I was hating it. It sounded like a Lee Harvey Oswald nightmare to me. In response to my astute follow-up question about why he didn't give up, he said, "Are you kidding? I'm too horny to quit. Being horny is my big booster rocket of hope." I think his manic cycle was kicking-in.

That young fellow isn't the only one of us who is living in a thick-walled bunker of loneliness and isolation-stress. Indeed, an entire army of people sits daily looking out furtively through the slits of their bunkers. Peeking out at the world, they hope but likewise fear that their eyes will connect with the eyes of some passing soul. No wonder there's so much stress acclaimed in this world today. Carrying those heavy, huge, damn bunkers is enough to constipate any spirit after a time. Horny may be a motive of those who have horny, but what does this say (in terms of motive to persist) for us older less horny goats? Oh, good--my order of Viagra is here.

Well, perhaps there is some saving grace with age, and that would be: the young hope for a lot and expect a lot; while the older dwellers still hope for a lot but expect a helluva' lot less.

What does one tell this young fellow, if one has to tell him anything? "Go get 'em!"? But go get what? Some people today still struggle to capture "artificial peak moments" as found in: have sex (assorted), snort a line, burn a joint, sip a jug, blast their synaptic network with LOUD anything, pills, drive fast, freebase an et cetera, "French kiss" a laced sugar cube. This frantic stretch is supposed to prove that one's lifestyle is not the pits, that selfishness doesn't "suck," and that "you see, I do <u>too</u> have a pulse!"

A great many others of us, however, have spotted this "artificial peak" stuff as a dark detour and just so much crap. Who says our young people aren't smart and haven't learned anything? If you ask me, they're working hard to crack some pretty tough nuts. What I wonder is: where's the mature modeling in sharing from us older yahoos? Do we have a collective pulse, a life of social cooperation? Okay... who took all the sugar cubes, FCOL!

Indeed, I am amazed at how difficult it is to find others with whom to learn the art of sharing. The streets, and city shops, and the woods, and the fields are full of good people who are, like us, seeking sharing-relationships, yet loneliness is a major social dis-ease of our time. How can we change this?

Respect of others and Nature, and self trust are the framework of sharing. Social value is created through the acceptance and recognition (respect) of others. When a person is able to respect others, he/she finds it is based upon respect of and trust of self. And the vice-versa magic keeps on rolling along: those people who trust self, also trust others; those who respect self, also respect others; those people who are friends, also make friends. And the beat goes on.... Can "villages" be far behind?

When there exists no acceptance and recognition between people, the Ice Age of relating occurs. A deep coldness, a lack of shared values, like an iron door, stands between us all. Whether we be relatives, long-time acquaintances, passionate mates, or strangers on a mission, nothing blooms and thrives.

"Acceptance and Recognition are the lifeblood of psychological life, or mental well-being and satisfaction," Martin M. Bruce, Ph.D. said. Dr. Bruce stresses the active involvement of others to afford us our psychological necessities. Since Acceptance and Recognition are acts, mutual acts of sharing, it follows that sharing is vital to our psychological health and mental well-being. I like that. It gives us both Purpose and Path. I equate acceptance and recognition to respect. Respect is a lesson we are well-served to practice and model continuously.

Robert Frost pointed to sharing with the lines: "But yield who will to their separation/My object in living is to unite." This unity was Mr. Frost's idea of successful living, as I read his words. Unity is an act of sharing. Whatever came of the United States experiment? Do you think we might rekindle this ideal... by... say... starting with United Families?

Our learned impatience, resulting from expectations of immediate gratification and pre-packaged "peak moments", has us on a short leash of perceived stress. We are confused by our social outcomes and we are poorly trained for creating more, or different, or something, or anything. "It's not enough! There's gotta' be more than shallow. Hell, where's the depth?" is a common litany in the "talk" clinics of America. Have you had your dose of "Road Rage" yet today?

Let us be mindful, however, that great expectations (early learned do not vanish easily) often lead us to great impatience: a moment can seem an eternity when one is in a state of anticipation. So we buckle-under to our desperation and we settle for the next "warm thing" that comes along. The dance goes on. "<u>Ora pro nobis</u>."

The productive activity of sharing is the answer to the ancient inquiry: How does one reach the other side of immaturity? How does one cross-over and beyond the brier patch of selfish uncertainty to a mature and creative life? The productive activity of sharing is the bridge and our way to that mansion in the sky.

An old folk-tale, if there were one about this, might go something along this line: "Should a genie grant you a thousand wishes to help you find joy in living, wish a thousand times to travel the pathway of sharing."

Another tale might say: "Being lonely is as to cut off a piece of one's soul and to toss it, in futile diversion, to the snarling pack of imaginary hounds which chases your dreams. They eat your anguish with a growling flourish, damn their eyes, only to take up the chase again. Being lonely never gets filled-up eating its own pain." Perhaps, I've just launched a couple of "old folk tales" for use by future generations. Tell 'em to a friend, to a child, to yourself. Productive what? Sharing where?

When death takes a parent, a sibling, or a dear friend who stood close in our life, it gives us a clearer understanding of what sharing is...or was. The sudden absence of sharing (of creating value) with another person is a unique shock, which no one can deny. In our attachment to others, perhaps a close loved-one or even at a distance with a favorite entertainer, for example, both people are as end parts of the same string. With death's rude abruptness one end of the line is gone...and the string goes slack. It is beyond sense or analysis, because the line, the connection, between you and the departed one still seems to (wants to) exist. Such emotional music is a marvelous cue to block-building on the pyramid of self.

Sharing is brought more sharply into focus by its stark absence as caused by the death of someone dear. With death the creative joy of sharing is gone, and no longer possible. Only the memories of past sharing remain. There is no longer any mutual time or energy available for the creating of value (short of psychosis, that is). With the passing of a dear companion the most valuable pursuit of living is more clearly seen; that pursuit is sharing.

A line I remember my mother saying and living by was: "Good Fortune is a responsibility to be shared." And, Lordie me, how that dear lady did share in laughter and song (she had a wonderful voice) her joy in living. I vividly recall how, when walking on spring days with her young children (there were five of us), she would point out a budding flower that poked up through the moist earth or she would talk happily to the passing birds as they winged their way to feed their young. She loved sharing with others and she loved sharing with Nature, but most of all, I believe, she loved being a mother and sharing her joy-in-living with her children. She certainly passed on a load of good fortune for me to share. She was quite a special and fun-filled dance partner.

A few years ago my oldest sister Gemma (She died in 1988, on March 7th, it was. We were friends for 49 years) sent to me a note and a poem. Her note said: "Something I found recently that Dad copied for me on a piece of paper - it dropped out of an old dictionary of mine. It was his credo."
The poem goes like this:

> A youth whose feet must
> pass this way.
> This stream which is
> as naught to me,
> To that fair-haired youth
>   may a pitfall be.
> He, too, must cross
>   in the twilight dim.
> Good Friend, I am
>   building this bridge
>   for him.
> (I do not know the author)

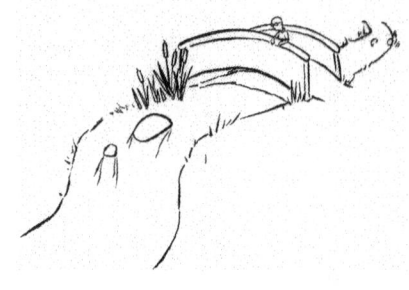

That poem reflects nicely, I believe, my dad's interest in sharing with future generations. His joy of teaching was in <u>doing</u>. My dad was a builder, a worker, and this productive activity is what he enjoyed sharing with others. He certainly built a lot of "bridges" for me by working with me and teaching me. I learned how to think, I learned how to sweat, I learned how not to quit from my dad. That man could work with the best, without a hitch. I couldn't have had better teachers or more loving models than my parents. Let's get started on that "village," shall we?

How often, because of our own immature enchantment with distractions, do we miss a lantern hung high on a pole, placed there by others to guide us through the darkness? How many lessons blow away on the winds of our indifference? How many teachers of whatever age, ilk, bent, or persuasion do we remain deaf and blind to? Only with the deaths of my parents, for example, did I begin to truly note and appreciate their lessons and their special efforts to try and share with me. And now that I'm a full six decades on this rusty ol' planet, not a day goes by that I don't at least nod in their direction in thanks. They're part of that ever-growing, beloved "Gang in the Sky."

Society, by definition, is people living collectively. Remove people and society vanishes. Society is not rock hard, damp, dusty, tangible, or edible. Society is an interactive state-of-being created, moment-by-moment, inch-by-inch, day-by-day, by a range of behavior, personal and interpersonal, that runs from, (a) cooperative sharing of people who enjoy its cumulative benefits, to (b) self-interested conflict in which Might is argued to be right. Fun to this latter crowd is: I lead, you follow. You handle the pain part; I'll deal with the gain.

There's a saying on the streets that goes like this: "You can tell how a neighborhood is doing, by watching the dances the people do. If they're all dancing alone, it's Halloween everyday." One note sounded alone does not create harmony in music; one person acting alone does not create harmony in living.

It takes <u>both</u> the bee and the flower in combination to create honey. Neither one, without the other, is capable of the feat alone. Regardless of how busy the bee, or how beautiful and fragrant the flower - no honey results when each acts alone. Honey is more than the nectar of the flower or the sweat and toil of the bee. It is a thing separate and of itself that is created through a shared effort. What sort of dance can you see in your neighborhood? (Do bees sweat?)

We humans cannot create the honey of human existence alone. The answer is clear. Some of us have been trying but it simply can't be done. Alone begets alone, it does not beget sharing regardless of how we strain or pray for a mutation of special favor.

As a rope is made strong by weaving the individual fibers, so that each fiber in its unique different direction proceeds, so is a society made strong by the interweaving of its people. Let each person develop the fibers of their cooperative character and their social values, then weave these fibers of Self with those fibers of Others who have likewise developed their social character and cooperative values. The daily relations between people are founded upon an awareness of and an interactional comparison of mutual and diverse values. A balanced and harmonious flow of these cooperative social values is called "morality." It is this comparative bridging across values that links individuals, communities, and countries together.

Homer (<u>The Odyssey</u>, "Book VI") told us, joyously: "There is nothing more admirable than when two people who see eye to eye keep house as husband and wife, confounding their enemies and delighting their friends, as they themselves know best."

How do you choose to use your life's energy? Do you prefer, (1) to pull others toward you and you toward them in mutual sharing, or (2) to push others and self apart in selfish fear? Common sense tells you to go for the "pull." But where does one get the tools for the job? Where's the "gravity winch" when you need it?

If, as has been said, science is a social enterprise and if we humans are, in fact, a marvelous tool-making animal, then Humanity in seeking to protect and create social quality must be oozing with potential solutions. Just as writing, for example, is a tool upon which civilization rests, and ideas are tools for purposive change, so also there are tools for relating and sharing. But the tools for relationship, unlike a hammer or a needle, are not easily found or simply owned... because they are not pre-packaged and stockpiled.

The tools for relating and sharing must be personally created using awareness of self, others, and Nature, combined with patience, respect, and humor as demonstrated in personal, and social, and ecological experiences. Sharing and relating tools, those tools for creating value and those for creating opportunity, are forged and honed and polished throughout a person's life time by means of productive activity. These tools cannot be borrowed, such as might a rake or a lawnmower. These tools have to be <u>created</u> by each of us for our own use, in our own way, as fit our individual temperament, character, and social-ecological context. As the person shapes the tool, so too does the tool shape the person. You want to <u>sits</u> and talk "sweat-equity"? Let's <u>sits</u>.

Some relating tools used by others are of such simple clarity and subtle lightness as to be missed by us when seeking models upon which to base our own creations. An example that comes to my mind is a line from a letter written to me. The person simply wrote: "I had a very happy experience today which I would like to tell you about." I was eager to read on - to become a partner in the event. Some people are masters in setting up interchanges. They say and do things in living so well that, if we are aware, we can learn immeasurably from them. And don't overlook or discount anyone; people can surprise you.

While you can't borrow intact the tools of relating and sharing, you can use others and Nature as positive and negative models from which to spin. Nature, which knows herself quite well, is available to everyone for relating and sharing. Even when she is as angry as a stopped-up toilet in Hell, or as abrupt as a frog eating a fly, or an alligator snapping down the frog, or as silent as a leaf drifting downward from a tree branch. We can learn enduring lessons from the animals, flowers, clouds, rocks, rivers, and raindrops to mention but a few of Nature's teachers and models. This is why we study biology, botany, geology, and ecology, isn't it? Or is it only to humble our memory for textbook names and to skewer us with tests in the classroom? Wherever we find our models, whether from the social kindness of a stranger, the tick-tock of Nature, or from our own imagination, the Dance of the Pyramids, as productive activity, is well worth the energy. <u>This</u> is the dance of a lifetime.

For most of us, most of the time, our sharing and relating tools are quite crude. In some situations, I find that I have no tools at all. When I find myself tool-less, I try to spot the lesson that's busily stomping mudholes in my manner, and I remind myself that since living without new experiences could be deeply boring I reach for a pinch of humor. I expect kinks, bumps, and snags--after all, I'm an active person. As I endure the stompings, I try to break the code of the lesson, and I hope that wisdom is not too slow in coming. Since I also enjoy a ration of pats and caresses in living, I seek to borrow tool-ideas from others, just as any aware person does. My best teachers have been those people who create living as a joyous learning adventure right to the last bump's dusty end.

The movie-character, cowboy-sidekick Gabby Hayes is one-of my favorite optimistic role-types. Despite the rutted roads and bouncy journey, a determined Gabby was never tossed-off the stagecoach as it evaded the hostile forces of evil in a mad dash to Medicine Bow. Gabby, dusting himself off after a hard-knocks ride, used to spiritedly say, "You're dang tootin'! I was born ready, Roi!" Gabby, thanks largely to the kindness of script writers, could gallop through the gates of Hell and back and never singe a whisker--we should all have such "Happy Trails."

Of course, ol' Gabby was but a made-for-movies false-creation whose reality was pure fantasy. The strangers upon whose kindness he depended were hired writers. The outcome of every episode was known, predictable, and safe. Optimism is easy to bake when using a kiln of steady make-believe. While our world is not necessarily always blow-torch hot or chain-saw risky, it does have its allotment of iffy flips and flops. "The real world," a jokester friend of mine likes to say, "has a lot in common with a seesaw, an elevator, a beerstein, a penis, an airplane, a frog's butt, a golfer's scores or anything else that has it ups and downs." As for optimism and pessimism I, as most people, view optimism as the up-side, and pessimism as the down-side of attitude. And I would rather live energized by "wahoo" optimism than to camp in the dreary negative-rub of full-time pessimism. I'd rather wear a grin than a grimace, and I prefer seeing you smile than scranch.

Don't get me wrong; we all slip into the low attitude-ranks now and then. I didn't say that I never go there. I said that I don't like it there. The pessimists think they're positively right about being wrongly negative because they claim to have sickness, death and the rest of the apocalyptic clan on their side.... Some allies, these. These dark-siders, these minimists, favor the echoes of lonely isolation. I'm interested in the social cooperation encouraged by optimism, maximism, and hope. Pessimists believe that anyone who says, "We're all in this together" is just trying to sell something for personal gain, and that social cooperation is only tapioca hoopla and road kill barfage. They like to hold that emotional muggers and bandits have inherited the earth--scammed the meek, no doubt--and are in ambush for anyone foolish enough to be generous with acceptance and recognition of others and Nature. But while pessimistic "pissing-matches" are not my personal choice in dance parties, I do feel an appreciation toward the die-hard, hard-core, camped-for-the-duration pessimists with their depressive harvest of fear and their endless "fondling of turds."

What do the pessimists have to offer in a gesture of sharing? Aside from hoarding most of the anger in a given moment in the universe, or demonstrating how depressing it is to spend life being pissed-off at their own expectations what do the pessimists offer in terms of created value in living?

They do offer a point of view, you're right about that. When things smell, either good or bad, they certainly can crow a lot about either direction. They're not real choosy about bitchin'. In fact, just as <u>up</u> would be meaningless without <u>down</u>, where would optimists be without pessimists? I'll give the "down-siders" credit: they manage to draw more lines in the sand along more opposite sides of an issue than most of us knew there were sides to be opposite of. But what I've come to appreciate about their efforts is: on the <u>opposite</u> side of every one of their negative ideas dwells a positive idea. They always miss this positive opposite for some reason. It's probably an oversight.

When the pessimist says that this world of ours "sucks," I hear two things: one, the agony of their own crushed expectations; two, a challenge to me to be productively active in cooperative social sharing. However, since it's unlikely that I'll be dancing with any of <u>them</u>, I invite <u>you</u> to join me to change this society. Let's trust our dreams, not our nightmares, and let's act our trust, not our fear. Care to dance? Or would you rather group-hyperventilate?

Several years ago (many several), when I was twenty-five years old, I was about to marry. I was a reasonably seasoned person of living: a college graduate, a captain in the U.S. Army (the military manual said: a leader of men, an officer and a gentleman). I had lived in several states and a couple of countries, and I could juggle three objects with acceptable confidence. I was from a family of three girls and two boys (being the oldest boy and the fourth child), with the benefit of fine, hard-working, socially skilled, purposive and loving parents. Plus surrounding me was a large, interacting and involved extended family of grandparents, aunts, uncles, cousins, friends, neighbors, and assorted pets. I thought of myself as possessing confidence, enthusiasm, a fashionable degree of wit, a modest charm, and a country boy's eager courtesy and sweetness (and I was a better listener then, than I am now). Was I ready? To marry? Yes. To share? Episodically, at best!

I had confused and blurred sharing with the act of "mutual getting" - you get from me, I get from you. The marriage survived for ten years, but due mostly to my wife's social skills, not mine. I certainly had not married to get divorced. I didn't like the disappointment and the loss of the marital companionship. So I set out to discover sharing.

The first thing I found was that sharing is not some physical doling-out of tangible property and personal-pleasure exchanges. The second thing I learned was that I didn't know much about sharing...but I was <u>now</u> in the hunt. As an adult in age, but not always mature in attitude and action, I was an episodic sharer. Mostly, I was selfish.... And that part of me that wasn't selfish was immature. When I danced, I always had to lead.

When maturity doesn't bump selfishness from our interactions is when the interaction is set up for "crash and burn." This is true in our affairs with others and in our affairs with Nature. The idea of selfishness and one-note dancing rings suicidal in all aspects.

Selfishness lacks Fromm's ingredients of sufficient care, responsibility, respect and knowledge: the four corner stones of his mansion in the sky. Selfishness, which traces to way Stone Age times, is a primeval "relationship" tool. Selfishness puts us on our backs when dealing with self, others and Nature. Selfishness is the "deer-guts slick" down-staircase away from Fromm's "mature love." Caring, responsibility, respect, and knowledge of others, self and Nature are the fruits and harvest of sharing.

While having children doesn't help everyone inch toward maturity, having children did help me. It didn't happen overnight, or even over a decade. My children have been patient and marvelous teachers to me. I haven't found any miracles for suddenly changing selfishness into sharing, but inch by inch, day by day, I'm gaining on it.

Now that I've been promoted to the grade of "Granpa," I see myself as definitely more generous toward others, more accepting, more respectful. Some of my golfing-mates, however, aren't as sure. But I have always liked children, so it was easy and fun for me to practice sharing efforts with my children - and it still is. But as they'll tell you: "Episodically, Dad, episodically." One mistake that I made for years was mistaking enthusiasm for productive activity. I'm better now at spotting the fake in me. Now when I want enthusiasm I watch Richard Simmons "Sweatin' to the Oldies." He's my enthusiasm model.

Where did we ever get the notions of, (1) to share emotionally means splitting something into percentages (%'s) of giving and getting (not to be confused with receiving, which I'll discuss shortly), and (2) to "relate" is the fast-track to getting most of that percentage (%) for myself? How did we ever get caught up in this detour of a "Good Ol' Boy's Swap Shop of Emotional Entanglement"? The signs at every turn read: "Let fools beware! Immaturity is taken advantage of on this detour, big time."

The art of sharing can be evasive. To mutually create value is an elegant pursuit, but the essence, like painting with lacy fog, can quickly slip-slide away... in spite of your best brush strokes. But not to give up, my friend, for as Kilgore Trout liked to say, "The universe is a big place, perhaps the biggest." However, old habits can keep blocking the process and impatience can rekindle the ashes of immaturity. Sharing takes application, it takes time, and it takes awareness of feedback from involved others and from Nature. The kinks and snags can knock you all over the autoclave when you depend upon the selfish wobble of immaturity as your compass. As the Raven said: "Nevermore!" And the persistent monkey of creative myth said: "Never quit!"

The hyperactive, myth-proclaimed book writer (the above cited monkey, not me), busy at the keyboard said: "Nothing worth getting or doing ever comes easy. Now out of my way! I'm on a roll." J#7,.!XR;3?+=....

Remember: the waves of the sea retreat as often as they advance, and no one thinks any less of its efforts. Strive to be balanced in relating: give and receive in the same stroke with equal grace, and sharing will bloom gradually, beautifully. But it will do so in its own time, never to be forced or hurried. Impatience doesn't cause water to boil nor fruit to grow. When our mythical monkey has an attitude of patience, time is all it needs to complete the book.

It is not only "better to give than to receive (get)" as the saying advises, but it is only through giving that a person can <u>receive</u> (as opposed to merely <u>getting</u>).

To share is to trust self, and mature giving is an expression and a nurturing of this trust. The primary reason we encourage children to give (exchange things, cards, notes, etc.) is so they might learn to share and to trust self. Too often, however, our lesson gets lost in our own ignorance of what we want to teach. The lesson of sharing and trust gets lost in the "swamp of the property-swap." A person can not share if they do not have the mature characteristic of self-trust. Self-trust permits a person to stop holding his/her breath in the course of daily events.

When I share with someone - when I extend my trust to another person in the form of property, a toy, a gesture, a hug of affection, a special card of joy or support - and I sense their joy in being recognized, <u>this</u> is when <u>I</u> receive.

During those times when you feel that you aren't "getting" your fair portion in life's exchange-maze of relating, go and <u>sincerely</u> give <u>of</u> self, trust self with others and with Nature. Your "in" box will begin to fill - you shall receive, no postage due. If you doubt this, take a break, put down this book and go check it out. <u>Sincerely</u> give of self and you'll receive. Be patient, don't forget the sincere (it means <u>without wax</u>, by the way) part, and do it. Just do it!.. wax-free.

In our human make-up both giving and receiving are fundamental needs. Humanity is interpersonal and natural in design, as well as being personal. The extension <u>of</u> self to others and Nature is critical to the balance and satisfaction of our well-being. As in turn, is the aware experience of the extension <u>to</u> self from others and Nature. Acceptance and recognition work both ways. The "Avenue of Respect" has directional arrows pointing in <u>all</u> dimensions of context.

When you speak to a friend of your dreams or your most private fears, does that person relate to, share in, and embrace your meaning and feeling, or does the person just hear your words? As you seek to "share" a story of special personal value and weight, is your friend able to receive what you attempt to give, or is he/she simply showered with the words? Does he/she share with you, or not? It is often difficult to know, isn't it?

And how about <u>you</u>, in your role as friend? How about when another person trusts you enough to tell you that special dream or secret verse? Do you merely nod at the words, or do you seek to be productively active by creating value through acceptance and recognition? Awareness of self can lead to such pretty outcomes.

In our post-World War II lifestyle of affluence and plenty, we (in America) have learned from wee-tot time that "getting" and "using" are our roles and purposes for existing. The greatest social good results, we have been taught, when we make, or we help someone to make, a profit. We have danced this dance over and over for the past 50 years.

Socially, this is not a well-lighted dance floor. It is proving to be bad footing strewn with many loose boards, and it is inducing a huge stress reaction in many of the dancers, young and old, the informed and the ignorant.

In the course of strutting this stage, we have come to view relationship, it appears, as an electrical outlet made available for our personal "use." We plug in, light-up, and buzz-off. We do little or nothing to generate the current or to maintain it. We have deceived ourselves into believing: If I can just find an outlet (a relationship waiting in Fairy Tale splendor), then, ah, yes, then my life will be unlonely and swell. Many of us have come to view life as some condition from which we "take" without giving anything back. This is a "frogs-around-the-pond mentality." It is not a good long-term notion for human progress. Rivet!

In conceptualizing relationships with self, others, and Nature, electrical plugs makes a fitting analogy. In the standard plugs, one plus needs an energy source,

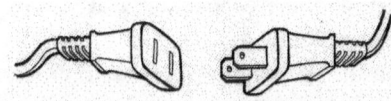

the other plug provides energy. These plugs are, for obvious reasons, called male and female. As I define human relationship anatomy and gender do not translate to a user-usee dyad. A frequent interaction, however, found between people, and between people and Nature is the user-usee energy drain. Do you know any two not involved in this draining arrangement? Nature has her ear cocked, awaiting your comment. Do we dare hope, or is hope no less a burden than fear?

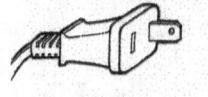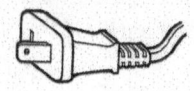

To visualize <u>creating</u> opportunity and <u>creating</u> value, let's create a mutual-flow electrical-plug analogy that represents the "sharing ideal" of energy-exchange and mutual-involvement. Plug in! Charge up! Mutually!

Relationship is not merely a physical act. To warmly hug to express sincere care is a beginning, not an end. Relationship comprises the value you hold for living, the pace of your social dance, the mood of your spirit: it is limited only by your capacity to relate (create opportunity) and to share (create value). To physically hug, for example, without a personal trust for embracing life is an empty gesture, at best. A hug that is seamed with fear and apprehension is a lesson in insecurity. The hugs that I prefer (whether a physical embrace, a look of approval, a friendly smile, warm applause, etc.) are when someone extends to me an expression of their self-trust. With such expressions is when I feel secure, fear-free, and I experience the condition called: Love.

Let's take a moment to glance back in review. In the abstract realm of relating and sharing is where all opportunity and value have to be created and translated into behavior. This productive activity of creating occurs between people or people and Nature in mutual acts. It is the major step in life's waltz. Check it out!.. over the rest of your life. Don't let the impatience of immaturity drag you on any detours of irresponsible disorder.

The more immature a person is, the more tangible his/her interactions tend to be. Clinging immaturity leads a person to honor the exchange of property, feel-goods, and creature comforts in a habitual barter. Sexual intercourse, for example, can take on an exaggerated level of importance, because of the <u>obvious</u> feel-good quality. There aren't any secrets to be found here. A person steps along a dead-end path in habitually choosing the obvious. Sexual intercourse can be an excellent, mutually created opportunity to move beyond the obvious. When created by willing, impassioned elves who are mature, productively active persons it contains not only a frolic of feel-good freedom but also a deeply perceived, endearing sense of shared caring and trust. A moment of pure rah-da-doo-dah bliss and grins... and a fair amount of heavy breathing between friends.

To relate does not mean to seek to impress, or even to always please, others. To relate means to create opportunity for sharing: the free exchange of giving and receiving who you are, what you value, what value you are seeking to create in living, and where you are located currently on the path you've chosen to create. It is, of course, hugely beneficial, in your efforts to relate and to share, if you have spent time discovering and creating information about self <u>before</u> you attempt to share it. It's helpful to know whether you are dwelling on the light or the dark side of the Force...or whence, if such be the case. The same awareness is useful in applying duct tape.

Sharing is not merely giving, getting, taking, or splitting up of material things. Sharing for the mature person is a creation of social value done within the self of each of us through productive activity with others and Nature. Sharing is based upon self-trust which permits each of us to accept and to recognize others for themselves and Nature for itself (herself?). Sharing with Nature is a personal expression of knowing self and trusting self sufficiently to experience love for all of life and its energy. "Amen!" so say some. "Ahem!" so cough others.

What sharing isn't. Nelson Algren gave us three rules for a good life: "(1) Never eat at a place called **Mom's**, (2) Never play cards with a man named **Doc**, and (3) Never go to bed with anybody who has more troubles than you do." So simple, isn't it.

But ignoring Mom's and Doc for now, let's look at Rule #3...not only as it relates to "bed" but with how it relates to sharing with angry, anxious, neurotic people. You can put all the joy you'll create in a lifetime with an all-cylinders neurotic into the side pocket of an elf's valise and have room left for the complete set of Nixon's Watergate tapes. "Never" is the key word in Rule #3. I pause... to nod and smile at Fred Allen.

When two people have similar goals in living but different values for attaining their goals, it is similar to two tennis players wanting to play, but each player using a different court. They end up not hitting any balls back and forth to each other. This is not sharing...this is not even tennis.

Sharing is not pain. It is not sliding down a banister that is wrapped in emotional barbed wire. It is not riding a bounding, angry stagecoach into Hell. In the Maximist's view of sharing: "When there's selfish pain, there ain't no creative gain."

As you know, people are like snowflakes - no two are exactly alike. Some of us are cheery, some are mopey, and some have industrial-strength depression. Some people, because they lack self-trust, put us on a strict Emotional Diet. Interpersonal exchanges with them can starve us to our emotional death. And how about those people to whom you react with an emotional allergy attack when you interact. The symptom is: you suddenly feel like "stale guilt." This is not sharing.

The more mature a person is, the keener his/her awareness of acceptance and recognition when coupling with another person. The immature person, to whom self-awareness, responsibility, and values-aspiration are mysteries, has scant practice in using acceptance and recognition in an exchange. Immature people are too busy "getting" to share. It is a clue to "bad news" when a person asks: "What have you done for me lately?" And it's the death toll of your sharing desire when they ask: "What are you doing for me now?" If they plug into you, your amps and volts can plunge to zero in a depressing flash.

Interpersonal exchanges can evolve as healthy, creative relationships or they can develop into deep sickness. Some people are emotional martyrs, but with most minus situations, after enough time and pain, the stick snaps and the exchange dies. It can die in many ways: in a burst of explosive anger, or in the dungeon of quiet desperation, or on the furtive path of slipping silently away in the night. Emotional martyrs are not models of maturity. They are only bearers of extensive time-pain scar-tissue.

The immature person will coax and bait their seductive argument that others are responsible for and the cause of the immature person's sour mood and bitter disposition. When we accept this offer, we dance way too closely with a "short circuit." A sanity tip from Algrens' third algorithm is: No close dancing with immature people.

Too often when coupled with an immature partner we find ourselves carrying the dead. Our journey becomes burdened by the neurotic carcass of the person with whom we are suppose to be sharing the adventure. The exchange too readily results in an "emotional" compound fracture - a condition that needs immediate remedy. We can feel used and betrayed, and funnel our energy into "pissed-off" mutterings of being mad. This is not sharing. This is wasting energy on bad choices. Choices made in awareless immaturity and stayed with because of fear lead only to bad dancing.

Fearful people cannot share because they do not trust self. They seek to get. A society that lacks mature, trusting models will produce people who become victims and targets of their own selfishness. In such a share-less system paranoia becomes the norm. People who experience no mutually created values in their interpersonal exchanges speak often of "feeling" vulnerable. The dishonest gap that stands between their private intent and their public act is laced with contextual confusion... and dread. Fearful people spend a lot of time nurturing their anger, and while they say "Love," they act "Hate (Fear)."

The full-time neurotic is uncanny at perceiving and at generating trauma in their daily affairs. They do not create value, they create chaos; they do not spin joy, they spread grief. While they may be attractive, intelligent, wry, even situationally funny... a "context-alert" warning is: they rarely put inherited and experiential components together in expressions of mood-setting, creative humor... or enduring care for others and Nature.

We should all be as fortunate as Will Rogers, the fellow who claimed he never met a "man" he didn't like. People, newspapers, television, and daily media flow keep telling me that society is a dangerous <u>place</u>. But society is <u>not</u> a place, society is <u>us</u>. Society is the sum total of what we <u>do</u> from moment-to-moment. Society can only come up scary when we fail to create social value (share). When we fail to share we are betrayed, fooled, traduced, and conned by our own selfish inactivity. Our worst fear then becomes our daily reality: we are totally, absolutely, and abjectly alone... and our sadness runneth over to fill our hopes, our hearts, our very pockets.

In our daily education we learn, more usually, the skills of immature competition, rather than the skills for developing mature character. Immature competition cultivates a need for blame when failure or loss occurs. This is not sharing. Respect is a rare traveler on this path, and there is no bridge to Fromm's "Mature Love" to be found in these lessons.

We all "hunger" for the joy of relationship and personal growth to be created in the interpersonal gravity-field called sharing. I am encouraged in my life-long search for my personal "Jabberwock" by this natural flow of collective, interdependent "common sense." Independency and dependency are frequently wrongly marked as the two primary outcome extremes in relationship. Independence and dependence, in fact, both place severe limits upon opportunity and value creation. Without relating <u>and</u> sharing relationship aborts. Interdependence is the key condition of community. And community <u>is</u> sharing: our most satisfying state of productive activity. The harmonious extended family, teamwork, cooperation, romance, etc.[8] are poetic examples of such dancing.

In closing this segment, I would like to present a notion of exchange created by my long-time friend Niall O'Dowd:

> You do not <u>give</u> a smile, you <u>share</u> a smile.
> You do not <u>give</u> love, you <u>share</u> love.
> You do not <u>give</u> your attention, you <u>share</u> your attention.
> You do not <u>give</u> hope, you <u>share</u> hope.
> You do not <u>give</u> courage, you <u>share</u> courage.
> You do not <u>give</u> trust, you trust...
> and through trust you <u>share</u>.

My parents taught me that the "Jabberwock" is unique for each of us. What do you pursue as your Jabberwock? Perhaps we can catch up with our Jabberwocks together. As Lewis Carroll wrote, "O Frabjous day! Callooh! Callay!/He chortled in his joy."

What is Friendship?

I put Friendship as a follow-up to Sharing because the notes for the two sections were so overlapping and similar. Many notes that I had filed in my Friendship packet actually ended up in the Sharing section. This says, I believe, a volume about these two concepts and their definitional interdependence.

"If the priest's coin is sin, my choice of coin is friendship." (Comment from an apprentice in living, upon his review of the state of the world in the spring of 1987.)

There is not a poem good enough or a song sweet enough to describe Friendship.

Schopenhauer said of friends, that special human condition and quality, "Between one and none there lies an infinity." Since the world is full of people whom we don't know and have not yet met, what a marvelous opportunity to leap across an infinity by sharing, expanding self and creating opportunity through friendship.

"Friendship," contended Soc. Prof. W. A. Sadler, Jr., "bestows communion that enables us to face loneliness with courage and with the awareness that we are not horribly, totally alone in our world." We humans, being social by nature, are designed to interact cooperatively. To have a friend requires that we be able and willing to share self, not be self-serving.

In friendship no one needs to win, self over other. Friendship involves shared mutual growth and freedom. Friends do not take from one another, they share. Friends do not need to control each other, they enhance freedom. Mostly it's so-called "lovers" who are into winning and losing, taking and controlling.

Who among us can say: "I'm a friend (to someone)?" The hills of life's journey are not so steep when one joins the trek in warm laughter with friends.

A friend is enduring and steadfast. In a friend you find a good teacher, honest and sincere. In a "lover" a potential vague memory.

Today couples often mis-state "only" friend as "best." When we are children we speak of "best" friends, but as we mature we find that friendship is not of degrees only duration: my "oldest" friend.

Much coupling that occurs in daily affairs is similar to two twigs twisted together by a raging storm. We hear this coupling often called love, and indeed it may be...since for the moment fear is wrung from them in their physical embrace. But are they friends?

When we waste our days on the whims of neurotics, a deep sickness is our broth. We suck it up with a straw wincing at the taste and abuse. Are we crazy? Are we so desperately lonely? Are we so weak personally that we cling to emotional cripples as our mates and companions? Can friendship really grow in such sterile soil? Perhaps we like to pretend through the tears.

Friends: when we are young those who discover, think and discuss, the universe with us: when older, those who create (do) the universe with us. What do you suppose is really going down with "family" these days? Isn't family a process that includes friends? Or have we pounded all the friendship out of the process, and replaced it with stress?

It's well known that to be world class at anything takes devotion and practice. To be a world class jerk or jerkette takes lotsa' practice. Why not practice being a friend, rather than a jerk-off? Like they say: "To have a friend, you have to be a friend."

"To like is to agree in value and purpose. To friend is to be of common spirit." Who said this? Do you agree?

The trust and honesty experienced in friendship are two of our torches in our walk through the darkness in living. These torches give us both warmth and light.

Have you ever read or heard it said that friendship is self-serving? I haven't. Yet, today many parents rear their children to be selfish and self-serving. These same parents later, as the children grow, worry that their children don't have any friends. Is this a comical contradiction or a tragic lack of awareness?

How about being friends with the opposite sex, is this possible? Some people do it, but many of these friendships began as young schoolmates who grew up like brothers and sisters. By not seeking friends in the opposite sex you reduce your field of possibilities by around (50%) fifty percent.

People can learn that they don't have to have a "sex affair" with every member of the opposite genitals type. Is anyone interested in learning this? Sex affairs (aka "love" affairs by the self-deceivers) are those shaky, but steamy, little liaisons based upon passion, sexual appetite and other fast-fade motives. Friendship endures the time-space continuum and stress hickeys; "old friends" are enduring, "old lovers" are used-to-bes.

In our fast-pace, throw-away, short-term-gain way of living it is difficult, once we are out in the marketplace of daily events, to make friends and share created values. Like darting meteors we zoom to isolation-speed, our fuel is high-octane fear, our destination is loneliness. But who can dare anything less? There are too many weirdoes, right? Most of us complete our list of "deep" friends in grade school, or high school, and maybe add a few in college, or at work. These are usually people we "bum around with," not "deep" friends. Then with our lists in hand (for the exchange of annual Christmas cards) we drift apart - at a high rate of speed!

Friendship by definition is a social term. We do not find friendship, we create it mutually. Friendship cannot be done alone. When a person tells you that they are their own best friend, you are talking to a lonely person who knows the straits of desperation well.

Sadler warned, "The development of deep friendships is difficult for people today because they do not know how to talk openly, intimately and frankly with one another, or simply will not take the time with so much frenetic activity that there is no possibility of sustaining much meaningful communication." Anybody you know?

I've never caught "unawares" anyone smiling while they played the card game "solitaire." Have you? Some may smile, but I've never seen them. Today, many people stare at the flicker of a TV set. They rarely smile either, if you've noticed. Some may laugh at the show or cheer the game on screen but they seldom smile (at one another). And how about all those "smiling" people driving their cars, or staring at their word processors? Isolation doesn't strike me as a particularly cheery pastime. And when it takes up the greater portion of our active existence the global smile-count plunges.

The literature of life's journey is richly laced with references to metaphoric darkness and small lights or tiny beacons of Hope. In scanning a poetry book you might encounter, for example, something about the beauty of sharing and the strength in friendship.

> Lift your candle,
> However dim and wavering weakly in life's wind.
> Guide upon distant lights,
> While sharing your beacon's glow with others.
> Two lights joined make the darkness
> Less hostile. (I made this up just for us.)

We can all become victim to deep weariness when after time and effort we fail to see a light at the end of our struggle's tunnel. Despair, however, comes when a person becomes aware that he/she is the light at the end of other people's tunnels, and that these people carry no light of their own. Life's dark adventures are less scary when shared by friends. Got a light?

Everyone gains in friendship, and the sharing in life's challenges gives us confidence and clarity of purpose. I'm reminded of the story (a cute one, I think): A man was faced with the uncomfortable task of pushing a wheelbarrow over the length of a tightrope stretched across Niagara Falls. The man looked over the gathering crowd of spectators and asked, "Who believes that I can do it?" A voice replied, "I do." The man smiled, took up the handles of the wheelbarrow and announced, "Good! You can ride in the wheelbarrow." Not exactly what the voice in the crowd had in mind, I venture.

Is this story an example of: "Two people sharing, only half the fear"? Unlikely. "Share? Who me?" asks the voice in the crowd.

As you seek and find others with whom to create value and enduring friendship watch how your fear diminishes and how your energy and available time expand. It can appear to be quite magical.

When I experience the mutual creating of value of friendship all the world is in harmony for me. In this experience, I know the wisdom of patience and sharing: it's pure joy.

Each of us needs to be respected, accepted and recognized. We do not need to be admired, adored or idolized. A friend provides us with the former, and can laugh at us if we demand the latter. Humor is an enduring sunlight in friendship. The warmth of friendship is in the humor.

Emerson said of friendship: 1) "Happy is the house that shelters a friend," and 2) " A friend is a person with whom I may be sincere, before him, I may think aloud."

I am encouraged in my belief in the fellowship of humanity whenever I see a person, upon entering a restaurant or crowded gathering, brighten in spotting a familiar face or when hearing their name called in welcome. Friendship is indeed a human gravity of most positive regard. Friendship keeps us grounded and steady, yet it lets us soar and frolic. Friendship keeps us involved with living.

I am not afraid for me, nor for you, for I know that we share a mutual dream of relationship. I know that relationship is not a pre-formed condition of imagination. Relationship is a process created by self through sharing with others or with Nature. Relationship is created moment-by-moment. I hum this tune to myself merrily and constantly, especially when dark clouds of isolation or fear gather on my horizon...and a low pressure front is beating the enthusiasm out of my attitude. Without the linchpin of friendship the wheels tend to come off the wagon carrying our dreams, aspirations, and hopes. When sharing is passed joyously around society's table, it's a pleasure to be a part of the human race.

A friend provides us with an awareness of self, and self-awareness is what makes us human. What a great way to spend time: working (being productively active) with a friend.

A friendly quiz: Who would you choose to be in a lifeboat with you? Let's suppose that it is a twelve-person boat. Can you name eleven living people to join you? It promises to be a long and demanding journey - so pick your mates well. Now that you have as many as you dare, let me ask: Would they also choose you to be a mate in their lifeboats? Ahoy, matie! Climb aboard and cast-off from fear and loneliness with friends in the good ship **Trust**.

Self: Who Am I? What Am I?

Thales (pronounced Thä' lës), Greek philosopher, one of the seven sages of Greece, B.C. 640?-546?, was asked what was most difficult to man; he answered: "To know one's self." (Diogenes) So the idea of self goes well back into the early innings.

I can tell Thales and Diogenes that writing about the topic of self is also quite a rub. Years ago, when I was either a lot braver or a lot dumber, I used to rattlesnake hunt in the deserts of New Mexico. The saying then was: "When you can grab a rattler by its ears, you're real good." To overcome fear is one part of it, but to grab a rattler by its ears you really have to work at it...plus you have to create the ears. "To know one's self" as Thales told us, is in the same league.

The rise in interest in natural phenomena, which signaled the end of the Middle Ages, gave birth to our current romance with science. Now we see an increase in interest in human qualities to keep pace with technology: we humans of the globe's western balcony are now looking, finally, at "inner space" as well as at "outer space." Several Greeks in B.C. days are credited with the idea of: "Know thyself." "Gnothi seauton" is supposedly how they said it. (It certainly sounds like Greek to me.) But these thinkers of old did little to tell us how we might achieve this gem of acquaintanceship.

Recent decades have been loaded with suggestions about getting to know yourself, getting to love yourself, actualizing yourself, being nice to yourself, doing etc. for yourself. As a result many of us have come to view self as if self were an encapsulated entity, separate from us; some mysterious shadow that eludes us in a "hide-and-seek" game.

The self is no shadow, no dancing spirit that hides in some crease deep within you. The self is you - it's how you feel, think, act, and interact. Be aware of you, and you are seeing self. There is no need for magic, secrets, or excuses. People who have something to sell, at a profit, are the ones who want you to believe that they have the secret to your self. They hope to get rich on your ignorance.

I have to smile when I hear or read "professionals" who refer to self as if it were a folded road map, with each of us having a tiny copy tucked snugly away within us. These road maps, they would have us believe, are waiting patiently for us to find them, unfold them and come to "know self" by reading the map. All roads lead to self, so to speak: for a fee, of course. Self is not some pre-determined icon or road map or flash of "consciousness." All selves are not equal. Has anyone ever rushed from their bath screaming "Eureka!" about suddenly and permanently finding "Self"? I'd be a serious doubter.

An important question is: Can the "daily" person, without add-on, extra rituals, performing and living in an ordinary way come to know self? Can all people hope to achieve this level-of-being in the normal course of daily living? The answer is: Yes. The means is situational awareness.

The self is not an isolated, one-dimensional, encapsulated entity. Just as Planet Earth is affected by the gravity of the universe and the energy of the sun, self is affected by others and by Nature. Every time you sense gravity's tug, be of the notice that you are not separate from Nature, and likewise you are not separate from others.

Nature is pure of purpose. She strikes no treaty, no promise, no compromise. We humans are not that far come from Nature that we don't recognize ourselves in her. As we have sought to control Nature, so also must we seek to control ourselves. We have been slack in this latter duty.

Humans without social dignity are no higher in function than dogs, cats, or opossums, which are slaves to their appetites. Not liking to hang by my tail, bark at the moon, or caterwaul in the night, I choose to be otherwise.

Uniqueness is frequently erroneously practiced as: doing what everyone else does but in a different way. This is being the "odd-bean in the jar" effort. Uniqueness is practicing elevated and creative style in behavior and of thought: being a person of social character. In our life span we experience few unique social characters, but we suffer many odd-beans. Be actively productive and create refreshing socially cooperative human-traits. Let others copy you, if they must.

In finding life's pathway let each person choose his/her own way with a personal compass of social value and cooperation. Let those who have gone productively before us, to be sure, hold their lanterns high so that we might guide upon them. But let us do so with cautious awareness, for what is/was good for them may not be good for you or me. As Robert Burns warned us: "The best-laid schemes o' mice an' men,/Gang aft a-gley./And leave us nought but grief and pain, / For promised joy." Gang-ing aft a-gley is not my idea of a happy habit.

Humans are not separate from Nature and we are not separate from others. Due to memory of the past, dreams of the future, and rational involvement in the present we create the context for self awareness. We living humans are in constant verb-mode. We are capable of aware motion: each of us can make choices and participate in creative living. To use thought in reflective, rational solution-spinning; to apply your experience, learning, conditioning, habits, motives, theories of being, and framework of behavior in contextual awareness is to create opportunity for knowing <u>and</u> understanding self. It is called, by some, "Building your Pyramid." I like the term and use it with myself often. Whenever you sense your verb-mode... turn up your awareness knob. Self, in one or more of its aspects, is humming to you. Say, "Hey!"

The secret key of any theology is said to be anthropology... or how humans project their own traits onto God. If this is so, then the key secret of any creative social relating and sharing is self. A major method in which each of us can fool ourselves about social reality (cooperative relationship) is through a flawed "projection" of blurred self-knowledge onto others. How clearly and fully one "sees" inwardly of self determines the clarity of one's outward "view" of others and Nature. A fuzzy contextual focal-length can give--Oish, such a migraine!

The keystone goal in living is to know self. In doing this we can relate to and share with others, come to enjoy Nature in its purest form, content and interaction, and we can find the hide-outs of God. There are no dividing walls in self, between self and others, or between self and Nature; there is only contextual mis-information. Each of us has to pick up our own "litter" here.

Relationship, as with self, does not exist in a pre-formed structure waiting to be found, unfolded, or uncapped like a jar of pre-whipped jelly and peanut butter. Relationship has to be created, moment-by-moment, between people, or between a person and Nature's entities. Knowing self is a necessary aspect to relating well and sharing mutually. The more awareness one has of contextual self, the more effective he/she is in relating and sharing. This is why Nature is found to be so attractive by so many of us. Nature has a comfortable state of self. Nature can and will dance with any offer--she's one big momma of a pyramid. Perhaps as the poet told us, "We're nothing but brute with a little veneer,/And Nature is best after all."

To relate-with is to be in balance-with. To share-with is to be in harmony-with. The greater the self awareness, the better one is able to create a relationship in a specific context. The higher the individual awareness of self in any two interacting entities, the greater the potential for harmony and balance between them.

If you believe self is separate from Nature, name one thing you <u>do</u> without Nature. You can't breathe without the air. You can't even be a pessimist without the sun's energy.

Let's shift into a more conversational gear. As you know, each of us, in our own way, has to discover the world and living; exposing to ourselves the myths we honor. No one is exempt. In the kitchen of life, everyone is the head cook.

"Modern we" have made it, seemingly, a daily goal to never, never, never slow dance with self. We are the Gingerbread people and the music is kept LOUD. A common altered-awareness comment is: "Does knowing self mean I have to spend time alone with my self, listening to my self, being aware of my self? Oh, no! Bum-mer!"

We spend so much of our life in the immediate vicinity of self it's a shaded shame and a deep waste not to become more closely acquainted. Why avoid the "now" me; why seek distance, rather than close awareness? Could it be true that our culture rewards only those who focus on the skills of competition and not those who seek the skills of character development? Are we an achievement-without-character culture? If this be the case, then it's time for us "fish" to discover the water and to set about creating a new pond. Do you think there was ever a time - a "pre-hysteric" time, let us call it - when humanity joyed to feel the wind and rain in its hair and walked hand-in-hand with self and others? A semi-long sentence, but a pretty thought. And what of our collective future? Will it be a time of selfish "care and woe," or time of cooperative self and others?

Two decades ago (one score by Lincoln's count) I began writing a book with a friend. Our working title was: The Hounds and the Hare. This was a book about people chasing the mechanical hare of material acquisition. A rabbit which they could never catch, but which made them run faster and faster in pursuit. Afraid to drop-out of the chase, they pressed themselves to collapse, even death. The relationships of these people ended up being two empty cups pouring nothing into each other. Everyone was on the skim, and stress was their common cross. The book got so depressing we couldn't finish it. Ah, what a relief. Hello, Mr. Bluebird!

"You can never tell who is hangin' on the thin edge." This line was spoken when a fellow heard of the suicide of a close acquaintance. Have you checked the distance to the edge lately?

Most people in the regiments of life accept the role of the "enlisted." They do not establish the purpose, pace, course, or cause of their activities and duties. They react mutely to whatever is dictated. They march blindly into the valley of stress. Let me ask again: "Who's in charge and why?"

An old barrack's saying goes: "Silent water runs deep / Big mouths run shallow. / Know who you're flirting with, / Know who your teachers are. / Know where you might catch things." The point is: be more than a snowflake in the storm. Know who you are. Know who you teach and know who you are taught by, quit being seduced. Know what you want to teach, know what you want to experience, know what you want to learn.

"Know thy self" is not a casual suggestion. It is an imperative; a moral responsibility of each of us as partners in society. To touch life is to know self to some degree in some aspect(s). But you cannot create relationship with others who maintain only partial, spotty self-awareness. The emotionally disheveled person, for example, is not self-contextually aware enough to interact in any continuous energy-generating, value-creating, productively active way.

You can never quiet another person's fears. You can only show them your own level of self trust. Likewise, another person can never do enough to quiet your fears. Each of us is charged with self in all of its faces.

"It is only when proofs are lacking that people try to impose their opinion. Do not let yourself be credulous. Do not let yourself be imposed on." (Andre Gide, New Fruits) By being strongly aware of self you will not be easily imposed upon or deceived, for you will know a great deal about others. Their opinions may visit but they will not rule in your court when you actively know self. How quick we are to assume that a person for whom we "care" or to whom we are "attracted" is "just pretending" to be lost in fear; out of touch with much of self and its bridges to others and Nature. The unrequited efforts to span the divide between a "reality of relative awareness" and a "reality of relative non-awareness" sets up "crazy-making" dancing.

Have you noticed the contentment of a flower. A flower is fully a flower through its existence. It is what it is; in its nature it has personal freedom (grace). But what of us humans? Where is our grace? We do not even know who we are (by our nature), yet we seek to be more. Such discontentment is not visited even upon a weed. We humans seek to be <u>more</u> than we are, rather than striving to be <u>fully</u> what we are. We seek power over others (a primary myth) rather than awareness of self (a primary living skill).

"To be great is not to be placed above humanity, ruling others; but to stand above the partialities and futilities of uninformed desire, and to rule one's self." (Will Durant citing Spinoza) Neither Durant nor Spinoza said, "Road kill has greater self-awareness than do some humans."

The idea of being able to step into a 'phone booth and change personalities - from meek to omnipotent - has broad appeal. This is a favorite comic myth - an illusion of the self-diluters that has absolutely no traction in everyday events. To be a competent person takes years of social effort and involved experience, natural study and application, trial and error, polishing and feedback review. Self-knowledge is not easily, quickly or magically gained. A college friend would step into a 'phone booth, remove his clothes and run around the campus square - with a bundle of clothes under his arm. He was a mid-night streaker...which, I suppose, to him was close to instant omnipotence. Thank God, he never tried to fly. I suppose he was trying to "reach-out and touch someone." Touch whom? With what?

Benjamin Franklin said, "It is difficult for an empty sack to stand straight." Self-confidence gives a person substance. Self-confidence puts starch in your frame, lifts your chin, puts bounce in your step, and lights-up your eyes. Respect and trust of self come through the productive activity of creating opportunity (relating) and creating social value (sharing), not through deception or dumb luck or magic.

To be socially aware does not mean to be dishonest about your abilities, to lack self-confidence or to engage in self-scorn. Be <u>Proud</u> of self and hold dear an <u>interest in</u> the well-being of <u>others</u>. This is the social aspect of self. To be socially aware is to respect the four primary isolators of our culture: cars, TVs, computers, and self-ignorance... and to move actively beyond them in pursuit of balance and harmony.

Our brain developed as a weapon, just as the Saber-toothed tiger developed its fangs as a weapon. The purpose: survival. Now it is time for us humans to develop our mind (the unity of body and brain) as a <u>tool</u> of social and ecological self. The purpose: the productively active expression of cooperative living.

As John Donne liked to remind us, we are not isolated, but we are overlapping parts of the whole. The whole does not exist without the parts; nor the parts without the whole. The individual can miss being fully what he/she is by ignoring his/her part in the whole. Knowing self in all its aspects is the joy-filled dance of living. It is the golden binding-thread of the fabric of life when others and Nature are recognized and accepted as aspects of self. Thales warned that it was most difficult, remember? And Thales, to my knowledge, was never a wimp.

Comment: The aspects of self as I've come to conceptualized them over the years include: the physical, the mental, the emotional, the spiritual, and the social (others and Nature). John Seed, in <u>Thinking Like a Mountain</u>, offered the concept of an ecological self present in us. For me, the social self contains this natural aspect, but I find Seed's term useful. In any case, an ecological self is intrinsic in our genetic flow. The person with active awareness of self knows this current. We are all of the total flow, not because the new physics says we are...the flow of life and energy creates the physics, not the other way across. Let me ask you about a couple of other aspects of self. How about an aesthetic self? How about a genetic self? If you have any sense-awareness of these, or other, aspects of self, please contact me. Run up your lantern.

Let's get to the task of discussing some of the currents of self. Remember: the choice is yours - at all times. You can take the bus to Dumb Luck and Sorrow or you can travel the path of Productive Activity and Joy.

The world of daily affairs tells me that the bus to Dumb Luck and Sorrow is jammed full; people hanging on the hood ornament, out the windows, etc. You can't see out the windows for the people, but there's no driver anyway...so what's to worry. On the pathway to Productive Activity and Joy, should you choose to go this way, try using the guide posts to awareness listed later in this section. And please write to me with other hints and experiences to self-knowledge that you have personally created and/or discovered along the way.

As I've stated, self is not some tiny sculpted statue hidden away in the dense mist of our arrogance, ignorance, and indifference. When you hear it said: "You must find the answer to life's questions <u>within</u>, not without," this does not refer to some secret stashed in a tiny nook deep within your inner space. It...<u>within</u>...is you! Within is all that you are, your activities, experiences, dreams, memories, relationships, your past, present, and future. Within is your beliefs, attitudes, friends, and foes. Within is all that you are, were, and shall (and will to) be. Self is being and potential to being. Therein lies within. The self - your answers and questions to living - is created by you. What you are from moment-to-moment, inch-by-inch, is where self dwells. Awareness is the required skill.

Each of us is a unique genetic and experiential mix. Our individual minds (body and brain) hold our history of the past, our sense of the present, and our dreams of the future. Self is the motive, energy and interaction of life. Self is the experiential and genetic sum-total of each of us in relation to others and Nature.

In our plunge into this contextual pool of self we can become lost, through poor awareness and fear, from others and Nature. Innately we humans are involved in our fellows and in Nature. We need others and Nature to continue to live. Self is social and ecological. You cannot know self if you ignore the cooperative (social) and natural (ecological) aspects of living.

The lowest level of understanding, it has been said, is classification and labeling. We currently do this with self. We label and sort when we don't know what else to do. For example, we are good, bad, ambitious, lazy, frightened, brave, etc. Labels. Adjectives, at that. How about some verbs, at least. This use of labels tells us little or nothing of inner-self. We stop at the labels too often. We dust our hands together and exclaim in elated pretense, "Ah, that'll do it!"

"Men in general judge more from appearance than from reality. All men have eyes but few have the gift of penetration." (Machiavelli)

"Nothing requires a rarer intellectual heroism than willingness to see one's equation written out." (George Santayana)

"Once read thy own breast right, / And thou hast done with fears! / Man gets no other light, / Search he a thousand years." (Matthew Arnold)

And how is this done? Self-knowledge comes only through awareness of the self aspects within the context of living. The art of awareness is more than fragment gathering, more than looking at the parts of life separately. An old tale holds: "To take a flower apart to learn what it is, you lose the flower in the doing." To concentrate on the parts blurs the whole; to focus on the cause, you lose the effect.

Then what is self awareness? Every stroke of the brush on the canvas of your being, every passing gust of wind carries news of self. Relaxed concentration upon the large and the small, the hard and the soft, the abrupt and the subtle messages-of-being is the skill of awareness. To know one's self must be done relative to something. You cannot turn your back to the world (others and Nature), awareless of context and expect to know self in its sum. To withdraw inward narrows and limits the definition of self. Without experience (relating and sharing) all inquiry of self is done in non-parametric darkness. There is no standard of comparison, no polarity. To know one's self a person must be involved in living, not a prisoner of some dark inner chamber, not blown passively here or there by the passing wind of unquestioned ideology. A person who combines inner space with outer space and becomes one with life and living has awareness. To put, moment-by-moment, all the aspects of self - the physical, emotional, spiritual, mental, social and ecological - into the whirling blender of contextual living; then to sample the blend and to know the whole, while being able to identify the changes in the parts, that is awareness. And that is an art. "A highly difficult art," Thales would add.

Guide Posts to Self

Now it is time to carve the turkey, time to discuss some of the guide posts I've found useful over the years in seeking to know myself. Let's begin with some thoughts about fear... and other things that Thales forgot to mention.

Clues to self are in our fears. Embrace your fear and let it teach you of self. To turn away from fear is to turn away from self. If we use awareness (not panic) when fear visits we can dance with self. Look behind the fear and you will be nodding at self. When I run from fear, fear keeps me away from me. Fear might be thought of as a fog on the window to self-knowledge. To look at the fear is to see it vanish in opening a vision of self. Look at your fear, see your self. To say, "I am afraid" is to label, and not enough. Look behind the fear to what you are truly afraid of, what you fear as an outcome. This will introduce you to self's motive....

Whenever you feel tears of sadness in your eyes, you might ask yourself, "What are you afraid of, friend?" The reply will reveal who you are at that moment. A good cry can be a marvelous teacher to the person who is aware. Go beyond your fear to self-knowledge.

I can tell how controlled by fear a person is by how artificial I am tempted to be in interacting with him/her. Their fear can grab me right by the throat, and just scare the hell out of me...if I let it. Check it out! Maybe there's something to fearing fear. How about fearing self? Is that possible? Anyone who can fear self is in big trouble, I think. Talk about a stress factor. The person who can fear self can never get a moment's rest.

Let's glide from the word fear to the word death, shall we. When a person speaks to you of fearing death, ask them to define death and to tell you exactly what it is they fear. For some of us it is quite a short distance from the word fear to the word death and back again. A person who holds a numbing fear of death will not understand it well enough (either death or fear) to speak clearly of its vibrations and paths. The person who can address death awarely, nod at self in the presence of death, and is not, in truth, all that intimidated by death likely has an interesting vantage of self.

To most people life, its appetites and pulses, is all they have, and to lose that life is to lose everything. Most people who do not live creative, full lives fear death. You do not accept death by thinking about it; you accept death by living a productively active, creative life. Is there a self-clue hidden here?

The fullness in living comes to bloom when a person, productively active in relating and sharing with others and Nature, tramps the roads and fields and scales the cliffs and hills of self-awareness. Attend to others and Nature but set your own rhythm. The idea of death becomes a yoke only when we fear the challenge of creative living. To seek supremacy over death is a fool's bluff; seek rather a creative and assertive life. Gardyloo!

A marvelous linkage exists between life and death. Some people believe that they possess life... and are the victim of death. They attempt, in this belief, to separate self from the reality of death. Death is not outside of self. Death is the backside of self. Death is not on some sinister mission, awaiting a specific pre-assigned moment to spring upon us shouting, "Ready or not, here I be!" We lean against death every moment of living. Without an awareness of death we would not have a concept of life. Life and death define each other.

A special human quality is: we can know what death is. An awareness of death gives us a deep sense of the value and beauty of life (all life). But ignorance and blurred awareness lead us to fear death rather than to enjoy living. A hint of self is present in your attitude toward death. Take a moment, now and then, to check it out. I'm not here to tell you how or what to believe and think. I'm telling you that what you believe and think will tell you about self... your own unique and special brand of it.

Once you respect and embrace your fears then social sharing can grow and flourish in your contextual potential and seeding. Fears are the weeds hindering a free spirit. Fear grows in ignorance - ignore and deny your fears and they will grow to dominate your life. Our brute nature dies hard in the unaware person. To recognize your fears is to see them fade. Social "mature love" grows in awareness. Social "mature love" springs up from the ashes of your fears. Know your fears and they will absent themselves. The absence of fear is what we sense as social "mature love."

Trust is a personal trait that expands as fear diminishes. Trust means: I know myself and I'm confident in my involvement and sharing with others. I do not fear them. Trust is a foundation block of Love.

The Latin phrase Vivamus ut viximus tells us: Let us to each other be true. But to be true to others you must be true to self. You must know self to trust self; you must trust self to trust others.

Trust is one of those traits which we project onto others, as is distrust. When we trust self, we feel comfortable trusting others; when we do not trust self, we fear to trust others. Trust is rooted in self, not in others. To love others you must trust self. Do you believe that you can be relaxed and anxious at the same time? Do you believe that you can love and fear at the same time?

Trust in self is confidence in self. To distrust others, a spouse, for example, is due to a lack of confidence in self. When the words or behavior of others bring you to say, "I feel hurt" perhaps what you might better say is, "I feel afraid." When you sense trust or distrust of others, turn up your awareness. What's the message about self?

Let's look at some other ideas to graze on. In life we are all historians. We are endlessly searching and learning from our pasts. And how about our dreams (and nightmares) of the future? What do our memories and dreams tell us of self? What do memories have to do with our point of view? What do dreams have to do with our hope and our despair?

In the pursuit of knowledge and understanding there are difficult stretches, as you have doubtlessly discovered. These trials will discourage the weak; stimulate the strong (Will Durant paraphrased). Any sense of personal challenge or call-to-arms here? Any note-taking going on?

Only the responsible person seeks to understand life. Do you agree? Do you seek? Or do you just _sits_? What does this tell you of self?

"The greatest of faults, I should say, is to be conscious of none." (Carlyle)

Be aware of the context you help create. Apply situational awareness to all you create and all that passes you. To remain in a cess pool is to be part of the "cess." Those who view choices only as passive genuflections rather than as active self-expressions soon come to view life as outrageously unfair.

If you always do what others want, if you always mouth their thoughts and beliefs, you show them who they are, not who you are.

Watch others, watch Nature. What you see in others is a clue to the social aspect of self; what you see in Nature is a clue to the ecological aspect of self. Self can be known through relating and sharing. The pulse of self-motive can be taken in our awareness to our reactions to others and Nature. To know self: Do things, then watch and tally life's feedback... awarely.

Time-alone, solitude, is an important way to discover self. Is self comfortable in solitude? Is self anxious, bored, angry? Or is self pleased? Being alone, without sound waves or motion, is a place to say hello to the "ego" aspects of self: the physical, mental, emotional, and spiritual, remember?

Study silence, when alone or when with others. Be aware of your thoughts and sensations.

Do you frown or smile when you are alone? Are you friendly with your self? Do you speak with enthusiasm to your self? Do you find your self bearable or ridiculous? How do your self and the mirror get along? Be aware of self when alone. Check your vanity, check your anxiety.

With each twinge or whisper of anxiety, with each delay of an action (major or minor) take an aware glance at self. Is your behavior purposive or random?

When you perceive stress, when self is tested, what are your feelings? How about that math exam, or the big ballgame, or the first special date, or being the target of religious, racial, sexual, age, etc. prejudice?

Samuel Johnson told us that people get best acquainted with themselves in adversity. The collision with ideas counter to our own challenges, nourishes, and helps self grow. This may help explain why some people are giants before they're 40 years old, while others remain midgets in their 80's.

What you worry about may be a clue to your values. Do children of the affluent worry over money? Rarely. Do their parents? Usually. What are your worries?

Sing your feelings. Sing, as the American Indians do (at times), with sounds but without words. Be aware of the mood, tempo, rhythm of the sounds. Sing your feelings...to you.

What stories were you brought up on? None? What games did you and do you enjoy? None, again? Egad, really?

When walking alone what do you talk to yourself about? What tunes do you hum? Do you whistle a tune, when you're glad (only)? Not when you're sad? Why?

Do you like yourself? Respect yourself? How do you address yourself? Are you ever profane or obscene toward self?

Do you find yourself using the subjunctive mood a lot: I wish I were...If I were...etc.?

What do you believe in? I hope plagiarism isn't your only ism. Who are your foes? Your friends? What language do you use? You can expand self through what you do and what you think. What you attack and what you run from... casts a light on self.

Thomas Jefferson said, "Nourish their passions, let everything bend before them, and banish whatever might lead them to think, and in a few generations they become all body and no mind." Do you create thoughts? I believe in thinking. Thinking lets me decide, choose, wonder, create. Thinking lets me be alive. Thinking is a dear value to me. Thinking in verbs more than in nouns, in process more than destination, in cause more than effect, in change over permanence is a joy to me.

To do well of self one must think well of self,...not grandly, but well. Remember humility does not mean self-scorn. The self-assured person does not hear criticism, he/she only hears varying points of view from which to learn.

The creative function, such as art, dance, sports, music, writing, oratory, etc. is an important guide to self. To be creative is an expression of self. Academic learning is largely an exercise in human history. When a person creates he/she always learns, but to learn (for example, memorizes the creations from the past) does not mean being creative... necessarily.

Come to know your ideas. Your ideas express you, they give you tone and color. Your ideas show your strengths and wants, your desires and addictions.

When you hesitate to act or speak-up, take a moment to see what you are afraid of. What loss or harm do you fear? What aspect of self is dragging an anchor?

Know your work, your pleasure, your leisure, your play, your relaxed focus. Have awareness of the milestones of joy on your personal path. What books, entertainment, or fads grab you (or un-grab you)? What are your sweets and sours, likes and dislikes? It has been said: "Ideally,.. play is the work of children... and work is the play of adults."

When do you think the best time (past, present, future) to live would be, where and why? You can learn what you feel is, or isn't, lacking to self, currently.

Who are your heroes and heroines? What actions do you believe best display character strengths or weaknesses? What traits do you admire, or dislike, in others? Can you describe your favorite pose or season of Nature?

What events cause your depressive swings or elation twinges. What lifts you up, what casts you down?

Politeness is not a social mechanic, a robotic act of courtesy. Politeness is awareness of others. Are you polite or rude? What are you committed to? What are your social causes? If you were to write a book, what would it be about? Its title? How about The Rub of Road Rage?

The music a person plays tells us a lot about the act they maintain. Music is often a cue to a mood. What's your preference? Your decibel level?

What are your prejudices? How do you behave and think when others express prejudice, in whatever form?

What makes you weep? What makes you smile? What makes you thoughtful? What casts you into blankness?

How do you feel and behave around babies, small children, brats, flowers, undisciplined pets, animals in general?

What aspect(s) of self (physical, emotional, mental, spiritual, social, ecological) control(s) you?

What do you talk about? Are you thoughtful? Creative? Gossipy? Catty? Honest? Kind? Accepting? Boring? Friendly? Do you fan the flames of gossip or fertilize the weeds of rumor?

What do you laugh at? Is laughter good or bad in living? What is the reputation of laughter with you and your friends? It is said, "If you know what a person laughs at, you know much of his/her character."

To be able to laugh at one's self in public is one thing, to do it in private is many things.

Do you have a good memory? A selective memory? I've found that most things I remember are not useful. For example, a college's tuition in 1956, the cost of a new car in 1975 (Ah, good! I don't remember that any more), the cost of a hamburger in 1951, how good a tomato tasted when I was a boy. What memory information do you honor?

In living, many people are like a blackbird flying against a stiff wind; doing their all to move ahead but getting little for the effort. A pause to rest drives them back, back. What stresses you? What's your awareness level here? Is something standing on the throat of your dreams? Does it have a name? A face? A shoe size?

Each of us try to find his/her place in society. We would all like to be like Little Jack Horner who "Put in his thumb and pulled out a plum and said, 'What a good boy am I.' " Little Jack knew he was on a roll, I guess. A funny way to pull a plum out of a pie, but it worked for Jack. How simple do you want living to be? How much risk and effort do you enjoy?

As I mentioned earlier, every dip of the brush can reveal self when a person is actively involved in situational awareness. Energy spent here is well used, for knowledge of self in all its aspects is the ultimate in human purpose.

Self, remember, is not a footprint cast for eternity in an ancient lava flow. Self changes with living and is revealed through situational awareness. Self is all dressed-up in context,.. and context is endlessly "trick or treat" -ing. Human and natural events are the sculptors of self, and awareness of life is the chisel.

Innately humans are involved in fellow humans and in Nature. The world perceived around us is not outside of us. It is what we are a part of. Humans are social and natural and need others and Nature to continue, as a species, to thrive. Humans cannot know self if ignorant of and blind to the social-moral (cooperative) and ecological (natural) aspects of self. To focus on the physical, and/or emotional, and/or mental, and/or spiritual aspect(s) of self is narrow, immature and self-interested. Such narrowness erodes morality and rewards humans with fear, not with self-assurance for the future. To know (total) self is to also know others and to know Nature. It cannot be otherwise, for others and Nature are parts of self. And self is innately interwoven with others and Nature. It is the mature person who doesn't worry about it and it is the aware person who knows how to deal with it. Know self!

Thales said it wouldn't be easy, and I don't hear any valid comments to the contrary in over 2500 years of human struggle. Know self through active situational awareness, then use this knowledge to create opportunity and value that will outlast the life that engendered them.

Denial, Deception, and Distraction
Are The Filters For A Blurred Awareness

"Gods are all adrift, and all we speak of is forgetting." So it goes, as we head into the 21st Century.

Denial is self-deception; self-deception is the death of self-trust. This fear is the thickest darkness, the most unkind hoax. It paralyzes us. Fear panders to delusion; delusion crushes the seed of our maturity.

Deception of others results in loneliness and crooked dreams. Deception of self results in fear and broken promises. Deception of Nature is suicide.

"The **BIG LIE** in relationship folklore," said Chicken Little's sister, "is: Happiness is there for the plucking, and you can hold up the sky with duct tape."

When do you get old enough that you don't have to lie about yourself or others any more? The mature person is comfortably able to stop at any age. I'm working on it.

It has been said, "A liar has to have the best memory." It certainly takes energy to keep one's lies in order. Just keeping track of what lie you've told to whom can be a major distraction.

To warn us as children, a nursery rhyme might say, "Lying is a funny game, / When I do it, I feel ashame." And "I wish I may / I wish I might / Have back the lie I told last night."

Lying is not done with words alone. Silence can be a heavy lie. Some of our most dishonest expressions are carried out through passive silence.

When I lie, I do this to cover-up a part of me that I'm unwilling to accept. I lie to hide a perceived weakness in myself. My strengths seem to hang-in nicely without any lies.

Lying is a social ill because it feeds and strengthens ignorance with inaccuracy - ignorance in both self and others. Moral conduct and social cooperation become guess-work and prone to selfishness when blinded by dishonesty. Lying can cause people to believe that there are no rules of engagement (as in a bar-room brawl or a Ladies' Day clearance sale.)

It is possible for a person to behave honestly but to feel dishonest. However, it is not possible for a person to feel honest while behaving dishonestly. For those people who don't know the difference, they have been betrayed by past learning. Such people can't separate their lies of behavior from their lies of feeling; others (that's us!) and Nature become grist for their mill, bait for their hook.

When a person lies on a daily, moment-to-moment, where's-the-next-sucker basis about who they are (because they have not created any social values to guide how they behave and feel), then the "little" lies of false-sharing (conning) come easily. How big of a lie do you live? What are your <u>social</u> values? This is not a multiple-choice quiz. We each have to supply our own answers.

"Some men believe that a lie told for a lady is a sacrament of grace," Will Durant wrote in his wonderful history. Such foolishness in our thinking can make liars of us all...but well-intentioned liars, you can be assured.

Others have warned me: "In the marketplace called America, everyone lies sometime, and some lie all the time." If so, the market will fail.

Trust is more joyous than the lie yet we seldom serve it. We project onto others what we ourselves are. Just as those who are open and friendly find many others who are that way, those who are liars expect others to exist by the lie. One paranoid always thinks he/she is dancing with another paranoid.

A major detour to maturity is a steadfast clinging to old lies. Lies which we formed in youth, and embellished over time. When a lie is so long with us, we lose track of what is fiction and what is not. Maturity cannot grow in the delusion of lies, so in the interest of maturity old lies must die. Die through a lack of attention, lack of experience, and lack of applause.

How? When in doubt say only what you <u>know</u> is verifiable, or say nothing as it pertains to a vague past of events, or experiences, or rituals. I work on this daily, and I still lie now and then. Lying is a callous habit, hard to bury, harder to kill. We have been taught to work diligently at being physically attractive to others, to the neglect of self knowledge. No depth is the result, as Flip Wilson had Geraldine say, "What you see is what you get." It all comes out surface, and washes away with a little water or time. Then "What you got, ain't what you want."

We spend a great amount of our time watching actors and actresses pretend. We come to think of them as Special, as Stars, as Idols, even, while all they are, are people pretending to be someone they are not. When so viewed, our heroes and heroines become myths, and our social models reflect the deception of hype.

We love and admire (is adore too strong a word?) our movie stars as the ancient Greeks did their universe full of gods. We see our heroes die (on the screen) yet they live (to make another film). Our heroes engage in fictional and illusory danger constantly and survive fearlessly in the make-believe world of film and special-effects. This is a deceptive world of macho bad-ass. It's easy to be fearless when you know the script and stunt men do the dangerous parts. In real living there are no set scripts and there are no stunt men to relieve the stress. It's just you and me and the Rock of Gibraltar, baby.

The deceptive personality does not make decisions well, but gives advice readily. If given the choice between being a classroom teacher or a school superintendent, guess which they'll choose. Or if the grab is between a donut and a Danish? Their main fuel is gossip because it has no strings, it is a free-floating, unclaimed "social hair ball." Many of our public and private bureaus are stacked to the ceiling with deceptive personalities... who live on "hair balls."

The functionally deceptive person claims to know every human observation, both yours and mine, past, present, and future. To test them simply make-up an imaginary, absurd observation, tell them and you'll hear them say: "Yes, I know that." Oh, another little test is to ask them to get something-anything-done.

The deceptive personality rushes from window to door and back seeking external stimulation. "Not having two thoughts to rub together, they wait for the train." (Robert Louis Stevenson) This flim-flam artist is a good person to place high on your "Avoid List."

There are so many "one-act plays" out there, it's little wonder we consume so many aspirins and suppositories a day. The game with the deceptive personality is: One card for me, no cards for you. You lose again! This is Nintendo in the flesh.

The heart of all addictions is denial. We are a nation of world-class deniers. If this ever becomes an Olympic event, we'll sweep it with ease. We are a nation of addicts and potential addicts and recovering addicts. You name the "whatever" we are addicted to. The list makes me dizzy.

In a society gone bad, everyone becomes a victim. Society is the cumulative result of mass action, attitude, and appetite. None of us want to admit that we contribute to the mess of the mass (when the mass is a mess). So we scramble for money, position and degrees - and for others to blame - so we can "pretend" that we're above it all, that we never lie, deny, or crave "hair balls."

Our mission in living has become one of changing the thoughts and behaviors of those around us (and farther out if we can get our hands on a microphone and a "personal ministry"). Women seek to change men, men seek to change women, and both seek to change Nature. This game, which begins as simple stress, becomes a full-time "control and power" neurosis.

Our current society encourages a strange interaction among its members. There exists a Code of Deception of being of different <u>roles</u> depending upon the circumstance, occasion, or setting. Such a code dilutes our awareness of self.

How socially schizophrenic can we be? We dislike, disagree, even despise perhaps a person's morals, jokes, ethics, and principles yet we work with them, we accept them as political or educational leaders (or a mate?). Politics, we are told, makes for strange bed-fellows - so does a life based upon Deception. Which person are we? What do we hold dear? How do we discover our beliefs, if we embrace our dis-beliefs? Who am I suppose to be? Do any of us know? Do we care?

A few people are fortunate in having a living or work situation that has a degree of honesty. But even here we hedge in freely letting others know <u>who</u> we are, and <u>what</u> we are about; we hedge by playing a role, rather than creating social value based upon self-trust.

In a society of deception, everything becomes a disease or an addiction because so much of life is done in extremes and excesses. We now have

Anonymous Anonymous coming soon to our life styles. Why be anonymous? We have the A-Z anonymous-es.

Every time a person takes nicotine, caffeine, alcohol, or drugs it is an act of criticism about the culture in which they struggle. Every addiction is a distraction from the life we endure. Addiction is highest in the culture where there is no common (social) purpose in the daily attempt to survive. Addiction is a result of sensed isolation in a society that is without cooperation.

Psychological isolation is the price we are paying for the deceptive independence of our culture, such as one person to a car, television's code of silence, and computer green and blue coma. We are wilting in terms of relating skills, and so we grasp for straws - instant sex, inspired sex, safe sex, social sex, junk food, shopping, buying, leisure, speed, drugs, action activities, and lying to self and others.

Our addictions to relieve stress (perceived as due to external events and agents) have become a major stress form in themselves - our addictions isolate us all the more. The cumulative result is: we have become a non-social, isolated society - which is sick!

But our current model of living and education teaches form, not function. If you speak of function (changes, creative sharing, outcome as a process) to the disciples of form, they will shun you in fear of your message. Form, which can never go beyond itself, evolves from the joy of function. Function is not a result of form, it is created by shared involvement.

Many people have come to view life as they view television. They do not see life as something which they create and contribute to and change with, but as something they observe. The message is: "If you see something you don't like - just flick a switch, change the channel." Living is not so simple. Living comes without batteries.

Distractions are a grave to creative expression. What do you suppose Michelangelo would have accomplished if he had had television as a distraction?

What we're into in this society is "Making Things Look Good." We make apples look good by spraying them with wax; but we've removed the taste. An apple that looks like an apple, but tastes like a candle is not an apple. A training program that looks like a program, but doesn't contain a soul, a spirit of fun, and educes nothing is not a program; and a style of living that looks like living, but has no social creation of value, has no "person" in it, is not living.

Deception is in every thread of our system. Walk into a supermarket, for example, and look around you. Is there anything real there? You might as well be walking in Disneyland. Are we still eating food? Are you sure?

Despite all our computerized quickness and high-tech cleverness, we have lost our ability to shape our personal lives. The illusion called science is in charge and our grasp and our reach, our lies and our stress are out of control. As a dear friend put it, "Our yellow brick road is made of puppy shit and yams."

Ask the immature what qualities they admire in life and they will tell you all the things which they are not. The very virtues, traits, and behaviors that we praise in others (our cinema heroes, e.g.) are often not the ones we choose to nurture in ourselves. Deception is a sly weasel that knows many trails to the watering hole. Ambush is frequent, swift, and deadly.

"We have a deep sickness about us!" I read in a recent letter from a colleague. He believes we are artificial mannequins of ritual: "Here is how to have sex in chapter one, and here is how to interview (both give and take), and how to be when at the beach, to take exams, to study, to be on the job, to give up smoking, to potty train your pet, and on how to juggle, and put in a toilet...oh, and here's a chapter on how not to have sex."

When humans start getting "turned-on" by personality (their own as well as other's) instead of only by body, then relating will take a major stride toward social sharing. Deception will be turned inside-out and stress will dive into a saucer of warm milk.

Do you want to see raw deception? The deception of our "dating" ritual could fool even Solomon. When people date, normally they are highly active, energetic, do many things together, and are involved in the involvement. In fact it's just too too. But they often miss the important experience of each other's self. The focus is on appearance and presentation to a fault.

Dating has a strong element of novelty in it. The novelty blinds us to the relative value and intrinsic worth of behaviors and moods and manners. If passion is afoot we tend to attribute greatness to trivia, hilarity to a weak pun, and grace to a stumble. I have found that the very things that attract us to a person, are most often the very things that later-on drive us away from that person.

A couple was coming down the aisle after their exchange of marriage vows and she was heard to say, "And another thing you'll have to change is _____." We say we "love" each other - and then we spend our lives trying to forcefully re-shape the other person. Is "love" a hammer?

When people "say" they are in love, they get married. When they "say" they have "fallen out of love" they get divorced. This is an exercise in immaturity, deception and dissonance. That is, since I want to marry you, I must love you. Since I want to divorce you, I must not love you. Where does this turn-on, turn-off "love" come from? It is certainly not created in mature sharing.

Divorces increase because we want living with someone to be a pleasant exchange, a relaxer...not another boulder in our already overfilled pack. High demand life styles have the highest rate of dissatisfaction, high divorce, high drug use, high strife. Is poverty such a life style? You bet it is. There is plenty of stress dwelling there. Drive through any ghetto or barrio...stress will bark at you from every corner. It may even chase you, and eat the tires off your car. Our life style has us locked into Habitual Deception, and we've lost sight of the social need for shared created value.

Every act of denial and deception hangs by a rotten thread. Don't hang your hopes on it. Just as to cross, on foot, a busy L.A. freeway is to practice controlled panic - for you are ready to abandon all calm demeanor instantly with the blast of a truck's horn and dash recklessly, breathless for the safety of the curb...so too is the practice of deception...controlled panic waiting to rupture.

We grow weary of the pace and stress of our lives, we surrender somberly as Hindu thought does to India's heat. We are so bound-up in judging others in the performance of life that we have grown fearful to live it. We love to observe performers but shy from the experience of living. We want predictability, not risk in living; yet we dream risk, not predictability.

We seem to want to be able to dance in the palm of an admiring, protective giant's hand - a delighted God of sorts. To have our life match our dreams is all that we ask for. We would use all "three wishes" (from the stock fairy tale/fable) for illusion to be reality. We want the line "lived happily ever after" to be the effortless norm, a reward for merely existing, a deserved, inherited life style. We want to believe that horses never die, that cats remain kittens forever, and that a summer day does indeed last a life time. We think maturity means old age.

Most of our daily activities are based upon rumor and gossip, both highly unreliable. Yet we search out and buy this deception. This is a form of tabloid, inside-trading neurosis. We are afraid to toss a pebble at the moon, lest we might fail or others might think us crazy for trying, but we'll dive headfirst into a pitch black well (a wishing well) on the word of a known liar (our past relating methods).

Despite what some self-help, how-to books might brag, relationship change does not occur by merely reading a book and memorizing a few techniques. They're lying. It's that simple. To try to create social value by reading a book (even the Bible) without relating and sharing with others and Nature is like trying to conceive a child through private masturbation. Why do we accept such notions of quick-fix? Involvement with self, others, and Nature is the path to creating social value. Practiced sharing and awareness come through interaction and social exchange, not through gossip, rumor, denial, deception or distraction. Let's clean up our acts and pick up the litter. Only wishing gets done by wishing. **Be aware!**

Oh, and remember: The prinipal pimp on the planet is prejudice. Just as confidence is a choice, so too is prejudice a choice. Make productively active choices and walk hand-in-hand with your Sense of Humor.

What's Context?

You cannot have awareness without context. Without context there is nothing to be aware of. The more complete one's awareness, the more completely that person covers the ebb and flood of context.

Humpty Dumpty might have stayed up on top of his wall if he had had a better awareness of context. Like Roger Miller told us in song, "You can't rollerskate in a buffalo herd." (Don't try, especially if they're in a hurry to go somewhere.)

One part of context is point of view. Point of view is an old idea first expressed by Adam and Eve and the apple. You can go back to the first scratch marks on cave walls of recorded history and see that even those folks knew that there are $\underline{X}$ sides ($\underline{X}$ being the number of people involved) to every story. Why else would they draw such funny-looking animals and leave them there for all to see! Somebody liked 'em, right? Did you ever see one with a grade of less than A?

Let me, at this point, give you my Stone Age formula for context (since we were sorta' back there anyway). I see context comprising PF x UFO x E(NO). Looks mysterious, huh? Well, hang around, you'll see. I didn't find this on a cave wall, but it's a primitive way-B.C. idea. Don't leap into mathematical gridlock. Have fun with it. PF is personal formula of life and for living (much broader than a philosophy of life); UFO, unknown formulae of others; and E(NO), environment, natural and otherwise. We each contribute, moment-to-moment, inch-by-inch, in creating context. Context is never static, and its total list would approach infinity squared. Which says: "Don't bother trying to list it - there's not enough paper." Oh, yes, a few among us - hermits, we call them - try to reduce the formula to: Context = PF x E[NO]. They try to omit the UFO variable (others) totally. But with infinity being what it is, it doesn't help them be anything but lonely.

I find Nature appealing because Nature works so well: it has rhythm; it knows its self. Nature hums: "Nothing expected, everything accepted." Nature is never surprised by its self. Nature is easy to relate to, even when it's nasty.

Horizons (as in future hopes) are not one per customer or determined by an obscure force of destiny. Horizons are determined by the individual. Each event, moment, or encounter is an avenue toward a new horizon for the productively active person who is aware of context. Like the man told us, "Confidence is a choice." Attitude is part of your PF. Create a good one!

A parade passes only for those who stand on the curb, not for those who have joined in creating the parade. They flow with the energy of the event of which they are a contributing partner. An accurate dual social-indicator of productive activity is: The doers, those who create social value and opportunity, and the spectators, those who "sits-back" and watch life pass. Context-limiters limit self.

Moving through life might be thought of usefully in terms of moving through air or water, or some such element of Nature. If you accelerate your pace without forethought or understanding of the composition of your context, be it air, water, or life, then an increased pressure and resistance can result. Your course and pace can become unmanageable... perhaps even harmful to self, others, or Nature. When the context of living is plunged into in awareless ignorance, it can be down right brutal.

We humans create our "perceived quality" of context. We have long known, e.g., that in the good also resides the bad; in the beautiful, the ugly; in the whatever, the etc. It is through our personal comparison of opposites that gives living its essence for each of us. Our perceived essence may be sweet or sour. To know beauty without knowing the ugly is impossible. Unity and polarity are necessary parts of our attitude, perception, and judgment. To the aware person, change offers the special chance to dance with the twins: Balance and Harmony.

Do not fear change. Andre Gide shared the notion: "The everlasting has no scent.... The loveliest flower is the one that soonest fades." We all fade, sooner or later. I have this recurring, sweet urge to mix and dance with creative folks who choose to mill along, and at, the very edge... of context.

As a youngster I took special joy in roaming a hill-top country graveyard, which was surrounded by a tumbled, rusted iron-spiked fence. Upon one of the headstones was the epitaph: "All things begin and end. This is what it is all about." It was in this graveyard that I began thinking about a personal context. I wondered who the person beneath that headstone had  been in living, and what sort of a world she (it was a lady's name on the stone) had created for herself. I read her message (to me) and I wondered. Though she died in 1874, she is still part of my context. That interests me. That keys my awareness.

We are often so ensnarled in trying to live life, that we have forgotten how to enjoy life. Our fear casts heavy shadows over potential joy. We forget how to find the grand in the simple, the simple in the grand. We get so caught-up in the "science of breezy speculation" (aka BS, by Rick Miller of Spokane, WA. talk radio, 920 AM. Hi, Rick!) that we take our human folly way too seriously. What happened to those cozy strolls with Humor?

Fear causes us to seek to control and limit our living context. Relating and sharing lose all spontaneity. They become calculated acts of security seeking.

"If you'll love me," we offer weakly, "then, I'll love you. Do we have a deal?" This is pure ol' crippled-rabbit relating. This is Dumpster Diving 101, FCOL!

With the rampant growth of our modern civilization (some call human growth a pox, a planet virus) we seek to narrow and deepen our trenches. Fearfully we hope, we pray, that no things large or small, destructive or mean fall close beside us to fret or argue for our meager space. "My love for your love. Deal?" it snarls.

There are those who divide people into "Hill people and Hole people: Mountain people and Valley people." Those people who turn their faces joyously into the light of day, and feel the refreshing wind and the cool rain in their hair, and those people who cower in the dark shadow of fear overwhelmed by the dust and the bugs; those people who listen for the meadowlark's call to the hope and challenge of life, and those who listen for the hyena's laugh and hope that this is the gun-lap. Do you feel "you" in any of those context-slots?

Who has the most to give? It depends upon one's context-perception. A great line is attributed to Diogenes, who, while in utter poverty of life's material things, enjoyed sunning himself by a roadside. Alexander the Great, so the story I heard goes, having just conquered the land with his mighty armies sought out Diogenes for he had heard of Diogenes wisdom, and admired the old man for his philosophy and thoughts. Finding the old Diogenes, Alexander asked, as he stood over the sunning man, "What favor in all of my kingdom might I grant you, Diogenes?" Diogenes is reported to have replied, "Be so kind as to step out of the sun's path." Who was the holder of the greater wealth? Whose perceived context of life placed him in a position you might choose for yourself? I love the riddle of this story.

Ah, points of view of life and how diverse they are. Some people choose to see life in memory "stills" - like a stack of old photographs. Others prefer to see it as discrete "flows." The "stills" tend to value the past as critical. The "flows" tend to value the present and the future as priorities. While those of us who see life mostly as blurred and out-of-focus we tend to value vertigo pills. Confusion is assured. The flow and ebb of living comprises a flood of definitions stuffed into variant context bases. What each person reports to hear a speaker say may indeed bewilder and confuse the speaker. If you want to talk about "being different," don't talk to me about snowflakes... talk to me about people. As people mix and multiply, so too must contexts mix and multiply. As people differ, so must contexts differ. Some people live a life of posing; others, of doing; yet others, of reading the last page first. In an odd world, expect oddness. In a complex, cross-context world, Awareness is looking at a mighty steep climb.

However, it is within the challenge and the pursuit of living that joy lies. To strive respectfully toward, to humorously anticipate, to patiently do, to be productively active are the aware steps on the path to satisfaction in living. A person is best spent referring only briefly back to past joys or memories. No striving or doing exists in <u>sits</u>-ing and reminiscing. A context dominated by the static past results in a context of denial of change. The past is useful when applied to the present and future striving for productive activity. Otherwise it is a vain attempt to stop the on-going current of life.

Is change resisted by some people because of a sincere conviction for the old ways? Or because of inertia? Or due to fear of the new ways? Or for none of these? But just out of plain cussedness.

In being around some people, just getting through the day becomes extremely hard work. Some of us can be such negative forces, and cause great friction in the daily affairs of living. Contextual sandpaper, in the flesh.

Even God is reluctant to help those who won't help themselves. This reminds me of an old story about a fighter - a boxer - making the sign of the cross just before the bell rings to start the fight. "Will it help him, Father?" a young boy asked a priest. "If he can fight, it will," the priest replied.

Seek your best environment in which to use your talents. Context is a major aspect in mood-management. "Each twig makes up the fire," is the old social adage that tells each of us to contribute what is ours, uniquely. If "Beauty is within," what is its substance? Simply stated, I offer, "Beauty is the outward display of a person's inward Maturity and Self-Trust." Beauty is a personal possibility. Go for it!

A personal goal of mine is: "To seek-out good people." To seek those people with whom to create social value is a great pursuit, a greater find. Open your context to many experiences. It certainly helps in creating relationship parameters, if you start-out liking folks. I suggest that you listen to what others say, watch what they do, and measure the outcomes they experience... including your reactions to them and their character-style. Some people create more balance and harmony in living than do others. Seek them as models, awarely and patiently weighing whether to accept or to reject their ideas, values, and ways. The creating of one's values is a process, a gradual, life-long activity. Go slowly, go awarely.

To divorce one's self from one's own constructs, in willy-nilly blind-haste, is foolish and frequently hinders learning, well-being, and personal growth. But welcome the challenge of change, for context-expansion is vital to relating and sharing. You are best served by being keenly aware of life's flux, and by embracing it with Respect, Patience, Productive Activity, and Humor. Practice dancing with change daily... or "sits" out a big part of living. How able you become at this dance will shape how fully you will create relationship, know self, and step along a living path of heart and joy.

Trust your inner beauty on this: Aware context-expansion is important to self-health. In seeking definition, I asked, the triplets, Smart Aleck, Thoughtful Aleck, and Cute Aleck, to complete the following sentence:

"Aware context-expansion is the soul of _____." Smart Aleck, true to form, quickly rattled, "Aware context-expansion is the soul of--poly-ethnic-funkalation-Afrojazzadelic-bluegrass-step dancing." Thoughtful Aleck, in character, pensively posed, "It's the soul of--gaining a new awareness of awareness in the taking-back of bliss from ignorance in honor of wisdom." And Cute Aleck, stylishly, grinned, "If Spam were the soul of life,.. then aware context-expansion would be--the soul of Spam."

I thanked them, put them back in the toy-box,... and I decided to wait to hear from you before forging a personal "vorpal sword." My "uff da" lantern is up! Your thoughts are invited.

In seeking interesting people don't sell short those to be found in the great books. They make fine companions and are often highly reliable. Be watchful of the gossip and myth that influences contemporary learning. Are we where we want to be as a national society? As a global society? Have you chatted with any of our "old friends" about it?

There are many myths in life - be cautious in how you embrace or honor them. It is said, for example, that a person cannot remember the face of another person whom they love. How absurd! How obscure! How ridiculous! Is that also to say, "If you can remember their face, then you do not love them."? What does memory of a face have to do with love? Bury such silliness deep in a well-shoveled grave; it deserves no more. Keep myths out of your context, as steadfastly as you dismiss rumors and gossip from your daily thoughts and conversation. Thoughtful Aleck had a point: We really need to awarely honor Wisdom... or Ignorance wins.

Shun gossip! I know this will reduce some people's source of information to zero, but I advise that they find new, more useful channels. Rumors, like mushrooms, grow best in the dark. Shed light on a rumor and it becomes stunted and withered. Gossip is destructive to relationship because it is never in additive context, by its very nature. Some gossip may be cute, but it is never constructive. Gossip is a brutal social-assassin.

A comment I heard recently was, "Most people deserve to be placed on a pedestal - they're all form, no content." The young woman who said it was, I expect, the victim of the old notion: "The people you meet, you often learn that you don't want to know them, and the people that you do want to relate and share with, you can't seem to meet."

I like to remind myself periodically of the idea: "People belong in the environment in which they choose to remain. We each develop and select the context in which we best fit, happy or not." Blondie is no smarter than Dagwood, just prettier. A relationship is the product of who is in it, sharing.

All analysis and reaction to work, events, and ideas have to be made in relation to something. They are made within a context, and this context, when fairly understood and consistent, allows the analysis and awareness to be much clearer. When a person has a murky awareness of context the analysis (the answer to a question, e.g.) can be more confusing than the original problem (question posed).

Many of us have learned to relate through food. We invite friends to our homes to dine. But our cookbooks have shoved our books of social skills, manners, and interchange to the side. We have become able to make, or order, biscuits, but not conversation. We have learned to care for delicate sauces or special wines, but not for each other. Our context is awry. We can eat, but we can't relate and share. Road-rage, e.g., lacks all sense of balance and harmony. Our stress-load has us enraged at everything from infants to presidents.

Our personal formula (PF) is the part of life's contextual formula that each of us can and do change. Each of us write our personal formula for living each moment of each day. You may think: "Wait a minute! I don't know anything about how to write a formula." You just haven't been <u>aware</u> of writing them, but you do. Whatever your formula is, you change it moment-to-moment, inch-by-inch...by a little or by a lot. This is your decision, your experience... your time in the kitchen.

How do others see me as I stroll the avenues, stand out of the rain beneath a shelter-shed, or drive by in my car (actually I have a pick-up truck)? Certainly not as I see myself. They see me as a stranger; I see me as a good companion. They may see me as unsmiling, while I see me as internal. They see me, but not in the same context as I see me. Nor do I see others as they see themselves. We all have roles in many contexts, but the velocity, angle of entry, duration, and impact vary for us in each. Life is a lot more than a cabaret, old chum.

Have you ever noticed how "point of view" can change? Place a penny on the floor, face it, then move in a semi-circle around the penny while continuing to face it. What has happened? Yep, you've got it - a new point of view. What was in front of you (except for the penny, that is) is now behind you; what was behind you in now is front of you; what was on your left is on your right, and those things that were on your right are now on your left. That's the way living is: while we're concentrating on walking around a penny, the whole world revolves and we end up with a completely different view of our momentary universe. With all the spin being put on living today, I tell myself, "Pay attention, Mike." You never know who or what might nod at you. Every moment is a special moment to create opportunity and social value. Ask those who know me and they'll tell you: "Mike's great at finding stray pennies." I'm almost as good at it as my mother was. Strays enter my context-awareness-zone often,.. as do the memories of my mom, my dad, and the "gang." My context is ever being written and shaped... as is yours.

"Each man's memory is his private literature...." (Aldous Huxley, <u>Texts and Pretexts</u>, p. 160). To be aware of this idea is useful when we offer to others advice, opinion, praise, or ridicule, if our purpose is to be understood. Too often, I forget to read the index of the person to whom I speak. When talking to a group it is even more difficult to get clear, specific feedback. This is an obvious point, and I suggest that you not pass it off too quickly. Keep the idea as a constant measuring-weight on your scales of interaction. Lift it, roll it in your hand with every phrase and expression, both given and taken. Use it freely with each and every person - adults, children, friends, foes, strangers, and relatives. Each of us have our references, indices, histories, biases, opinions... some of which are unchallenged myth. If your purpose is to be effective in interacting, you are wise to accept Huxley's idea of a "private literature" and to permit it to assist you. When I shape my concept-expressions to fit with a person's manner, character and informational make-up is when I have the greatest probability of being understood. I try to be courteous but unique, accepting but excepting.

"If you hang 'round the pond, ya' gotta' croak like the frogs," is a grandfather's old saying to warn against cloning one's character. It is testimony to the strength of context on influencing our personality and behavior. If you think peer-pressure is tough on character, how about companion-stress? Here's a scary thought:" The game of life is a game that must be played." An even scarier one is: "In the game of life every person is a first-team player."

The appropriate context is vital to permit an effective relationship in social cooperation to develop through a mutually creative effort. Consider how useless the light bulb would have been without controlled electricity. Without context harmony and balance we either burn-out or we never turn-on. Please, play the game of life as well as possible by having self-awareness as a major part of your "game plan."

Many of us, your teammates, are interested in your performing well.

"A living person is a bridge between the past and the future, holding within him/herself the dead, the living, and the unborn." (A paraphrase from Kazantzakis: <u>A Modern Day Odyssey</u>.) Humanity is a context of <u>time</u>, and Nature is a context of <u>space</u>. Human-Nature is a <u>time-space</u>-continuum creation to which we each contribute, uniquely. By having our minds, moods, fingers, and toes variously located in different Time Zones and ZIP Codes we create the confusion of individual human perspective.

"Are the aardvark and the zebra alike or are they different?" is the question. "It depends upon your point of view," is the answer...right? The answer depends upon a person's basis of comparison. When a lady was asked, "Is your husband a nice man?" She replied, "It depends upon whether you're married to him." She knew him in a different context than did others. Seek to enjoy the prose and poetry of other's "private literature."

Nobody is <u>wrong</u> when it comes to point of view. But some points of view do work a lot better in particular situations than others do. I have, in the past, favored my point of view, stubbornly. But I'm getting better about letting effective wisdom influence my ignorance. I no longer need to foolishly attempt to capture Bliss in artificial bonds of Folly's duct tape and Velcro wrap. I know that the Key to my Kingdom of Joy is not a Viagra-induced erection. My point of view is changing. I've decided against fear: Age and experience should be liberating, not entrapping.

"Our unique points of view," a friend offered, "is why the Bible has been around so long. It can be interpreted in a jillion different ways, depending on the point of view of the reader." We help create our context; we're part of the formula. Heck, Pogo, we're not <u>just</u> the enemy,.. we're also the human-component representatives in the time-space continua of living. Such a deal!

And we know that "each generation criticizes the unconscious assumptions made by its parents. It may not assent to them, but it brings them out in the open." (unknown quoted ref.) Our parents' contexts can cast a shadow of inflexibility over our own personal perceptions and point of view. At times it's hard to know who created your attitudes. It is only with experience and feedback-awareness that each of us comes to terms of sorting our own personal Point of View. Some old standards you choose to keep, some you trade in, some you trash.

In terms of behavior people will often attempt to establish a desired emotional tone by re-establishing old situations or cues. For example, high school reunions do this; or an Eggs Benedict breakfast was great fun with friends in college, so why not try it with a "shack-up" date. You wonder what you forgot to include when it's not the same. It shouldn't be the same - the context is different. Not just the setting and the people, but the purpose has changed. Be wary of trying to get old contexts to hitch-a-ride on present involvements. Contexts are created moment-to-moment, inch-by-inch so keep your ideas and enthusiasm up-dated.

I have read: "It is not what you know, but what you <u>understand</u> that is essential to good living." And I agree, but add, "It is only from within a context that understanding is drawn and measured." Understanding is relative to the total context in which the event occurs. The expression "You are taking it out of context" means that you have removed the possibility for (mutual) understanding of the issues being reviewed. Some say, "Necessity is the Mother of Invention (in science)." I don't know if it's the "Mother of" - but Necessity does provide a context in which the research and creativity can be more clearly understood. The greater one's context-awareness the greater the probability of personal understanding.

Mutual context-awareness is critical to all statements, events, and actions, if joint understanding is the purpose of the exchange. For example, a question "out of context" is idle. It is better not asked, if asked only to make noise. When a difference in context-awareness is present between the questioner and the answerer, joint-understanding diminishes in inverse proportion - large difference, small joint-understanding.

The context in which we meet a person changes our interaction with him/her. A male clerk in a department store, e.g., may engage a female customer in conversation, even be friendly; yet the same male, if a fellow customer of the lady , may find such light conversation a bit more sticky. The male has not changed, but the context has, his role has, her perception has...she has changed, as he has assumed a different role.

We rarely view ourselves as being "behind the times" when we refuse an idea or concept. However, we will humble to recognize on rare occasion that someone we know (A spouse, perhaps? Oh, God! Say it isn't so!) may have been "ahead" of his/her time with a concept or idea. We may say others are "forward thinking," but we are unlikely to note that we ourselves on the same issue are "backward thinking."

Animals are said not to abstract, humans, I'm told, do: with some doing it much better than others. A personal ability and interest in abstracting is useful in establishing the parameters of a context. Did you ever wonder what an unhatched chick must think about? Do you suppose it ever once ponders what the outside of the shell looks like? You'll have to agree, that the outside of the egg would be difficult for the unhatched chick to visualize. Assuming that a curious chick wants to know about a shell's outside shape, the chick must study the conformation of the dark, concave inside, then abstract creatively to the lighted, convex exterior. With neither light nor convex being within his/her realm of experience our curious chick would have to create them: blindly, with no assurances, no feedback, or hint of correctness. I expect that is why most chicks don't bother. But we humans do bother with such problems and the better we get at abstracting the better our grasp of context will be. Working in the dark is the nature of creating. If a human baby upon passing through the vaginal canal says, "Quick give me paper and pen!" or "Boy, do I have a story to tell you!" you've got a creative, aware one.

We humans are strange puzzles; we seek constants while we live-in and experience a complexity of interacting variables. William James warned, "A bucket of water drawn, regardless of the controls and the meticulous methods, from a flowing river - is not the river, nor does it accurately represent the nature of the river." We are best served to look to the broad view, the view that flows and changes, the situational context. Heraclitus, Greek philosopher, advised, "You cannot step twice into the same river." He might be pleased to know that I don't even try to step twice into the same puddle... or pile.

You cannot take, or force, or wish old friends, or anybody, into new dimensions; they have to join you there of their own accord, gravitation and creativity. Do not expect others to be in a context in which they are not. Seek to meet and respect others in their own words and within their own context...as best you can. Context-awareness is key to productive activity.

Despair is when you grow tired of smiling at bad vibrations, but don't know what else to do. You will know that you have camped in a mis-fit context when all your sun rises come up purple. Within the boundary of despair the market place is full of bad-mouthing "flies"... each right, in his/her own way. Is there a dance choice here? Is the "sun dog" playing your song? Attend well to the music that dwells in your context, and in the context of loved ones and strangers, for its influence is quite demanding. As Daniel O'Connell has so succinctly stated its contextual charm, "Let me write the songs of a nation, and I care not who makes its laws."

The work place is a major part of our daily context. In selecting a career it is usually urged by the elders and experts that a person find in himself/herself those things which they enjoy or for which they have a passion, then strive for that setting where such events flow. Or as my friend "Skeeter's" dad told him, "If you don't like dealing in sin, don't become a minister."

The value in using the best equipment in sports or activities to maximize the performance-outcome has long been common knowledge. Does it not make equal sense to use the best tools in the critical event of relationship? In order to maximize our performance in daily life we need to work to create the <u>best possible context</u>. Some created opportunities do not have a good outcome because of a poor context. Some interchanges do not progress because under the existing conditions a person does not have much of a chance at good performance outcome. This is not to endorse excuses, this is to minimize negative variables, where and when possible.

No matter what it is that you want to do, to do it well requires a conducive context. Be it talking with a child, having a romantic dinner with a special friend, reading a poem before an audience, strolling in a spring-kissed park - the best results come from the best context. Too often we try to force an idea or a desire upon the wrong context. The dreamt of outcomes are weakened or destroyed by the poor blending of events and aspects of the total context. Learning to read context, to reduce frustration, is a skill to be worked at constantly. The best of intentions can be swept away in unfavorable circumstances. Making choices (context-management) is the pulse of living. Situational awareness of context is the lifeblood of a balanced and harmonious beat.

If you move a relationship into roles of exchange in which one or both parties do not feel natural and comfortable (for example, move a friendship to a sexual affair),the relationship may dissolve, explode, or otherwise fragment into negative force-fields or ugly stress: contextual stress. People who dwell in a deceptive/artificial context soon discover that there is no joy on the "stress express."

"Be involved in the task at hand" is good advice. When with a friend, don't be thinking of some other involvement you would rather be doing. When walking or jogging, enjoy it; don't rush to finish in anticipation of later events. You dissipate effect, you diminish outcome by not focusing upon what you are doing in **NOW's** context. When you listen, listen actively.

Matthew Carney, writer and renowned Pamplona bull runner, told us, "In a bull run, the man nearest the bull always runs the hardest." The context dictates (in fact, <u>includes</u>) motive. So seek a context that inspires your passion to create social value. Get in the run, create...and as ol' Satch Paige told us, "Don't look back 'cause something (the bulls?) may be catchin' up."

There are no distances in the dimensions of context. No one is ahead or behind. One person's context is different from that of others in terms of each person's ability and skills to understand the concepts created and present within the given context. If you do not grasp the concepts, in the same way as others do, then you are in a different - however similar it may appear - context than they are. Context is not solely the physical circumstances. Context is every factor you can imagine, and some you cannot imagine. The more aware you are the better your grasp of varied contexts.

When times get rough people will often reach into their past to find a sense of reassurance. Nostalgia becomes a habit, much as reaching back to pat your wallet (men only) in a hip pocket, when in a crowd, is a habit. In both cases we reach back to get the assurance that something is still there. We seek to know, continually, that our constructs for living are more than frail bubbles. Personally I like for my contexts to have some predictability and my constructs to be more stable than swamp gas in a stiff wind. That may be why I pat myself on the butt so often.

Our context of living is a flux of change; a rolling wheel of fog and mist. When you think about the past, that occurs in the present. All thinking happens <u>now</u>. You never dwell <u>on</u> the past <u>in</u> the past, but only in the present. And as you past-dwell in the present you influence the future context in which you are in the flux of approaching (endlessly). Like the song says, "That ol' wheel just keeps on turnin'." Or is it "The beat goes on"?

Speaking of flowers (which we weren't, but which we shall), life is like a rose. Some of its parts are thorns, harsh, and forbidding; other parts are soft and fragrant, inviting the touch to a cheek or a kiss, gentle and forgiving. One part does not occur without the other. It take all the parts - the gracious parts and the less-tender parts - to make a rose. Is life any different? How elementary is life <u>really</u>, dear Sherlock?

If a rose is beautiful only as held so by humanity, (Nature has no such index or bias) then is any event in itself sad, or glad, or any what? Or do these qualities come from the perceiver? If a perceiver can know "sad," that perceiver, by the Law of Contrasts, must know "glad" as well...and the perceiver can choose which quality he/she wants an event to have. So "stress" is in the perception, and the determination of the quality of a context is within the perceiver, not within the event perceived. Ah, another choice. "A rather elementary choice," Holmes might argue.

I choose simply not to become so fond of living, or so fearful of death that I will whimper and seek to cling to life above all social value. Life is best clung to as a tree clings to its leaves. How beautifully it wears them in their time, but when the leaves' season has passed, they fall away. Change is natural. I choose to keep my context expanding and to deal in truth (trust change) freely. When my days are done and my context-awareness slips to zero, I hope the winds of change will accept my ashes as a gift, not as a burden. When the "gang in the sky" welcome me to their ranks, I will respect the invitation with a smile.

Such hopes do not have to end in a context of tears. The aware life is not merely a vineyard of fear, or a graveyard for optimism gone sour. To visit this concept is to visit self. Dance with it, once around the floor. What measure does this awareness take for or against us? Is it only for appetites that we act? Or do we also act for the simple joy of will? To will is to hope. To hope is to do. To do is to create opportunity and value in an expanding context. Hope has no tone of guarantee. Some may ask, "How can I act, if I don't know where I am going?" My reply is, "How can you know where you are going, if you don't act?" It has been said many times in many different ways that life does not wait for the best prepared; it embraces the doer. And the doer embraces life. Opportunity and value are created by each of us, they do not stroll periodically by our front gates. Opportunity and value do not wait in the deep parts of life's stream for a few lucky ones of us. So, hope is not something that we have, it is something that we do. Context is not something that we simply find, it is something that we help create through our actions and our perceptions. And fear holds no special claim to every dance on your card. It's your context.

Self-knowledge and situational awareness give a person an "edge" in creating a contextual perception of comfort, control, choices, and "giddy-up." Get in game! Stay in the game! Deal 'em! And never "pass the buck!"

Communicative Relating: What's in a Word?

Let's take a look at communications, keeping in mind that we are dealing with complex human behavior. This section will not be like the history of some aspect of human creation, such as political and military intelligence with its chronology and sequencing of events. Don't expect order, expect ideas.

The pro's and the pundits have been, for decades, advising people who are experiencing relationship poverty: "You need to communicate. Improve your communications with others." The question is: "How do you do that if you, or the others you know, don't have anything to 'communicate' most of the time?"

Like the saying tells us: "If you don't have a message, you don't have a mission. And if you don't have a mission, you won't have a message." If you aren't <u>doing</u> living, what's to talk about? How about peanut butter? I overheard, for over thirteen miles while riding a city bus when I was in high school, two ladies talk of eating peanut butter . I was glad to come to my stop. A thirsty ride. Those ladies may still be at it...forty-some years later.

Nowhere in this book am I attempting to define absolutely for you sharing, or giving, or receiving, or fear, or relating, or etc. I am trying to influence you to look into your own exchanges in living, your own creation of values, and to get in touch with, become aware of, <u>your</u> feeling, <u>your</u> sense, that might be situationally labeled by <u>you</u> as sharing, or joy, or love, or anger, or fear, or productive activity, or etc.

Words that are molded and cast, by past generations, and handed down from one time-space context to another can confuse, rather than communicate. When defining emotional feelings, as opposed to material objects, e.g., words take on meaning based upon an individual's experience and created social value. Don't cheat self of its full potential: get informed by being aware, define self by doing. Learn from the past, don't be mis-led by the past. Awareness Alert!

Too often in living we are like an inattentive, hung-over spider, and we end-up caught in our own web. We seek to define feelings with words, hoping to better communicate feelings. But in a few generations of awareless, reflexive use of "hand-me-down" words, our definitions start to confuse us and blur our messages. The words then dictate to us stereotypes, rather than assisting us in understanding a feeling, its personal nuances, its subtle self-aspects. We have dictionaries stuffed with words, of which it is fair to ask: "What were the creators of all the words trying to convey and why?" If we are unique individuals, then are we not unique in all aspects of self? So then the word "anger," for example, as widely defined can only approximate, at best, my piqued, personal feeling. Unless, of course, I come to act-out the definition of the word as my culture has taught me. Then the cultural definition is driving my feeling-expression... and I am merely a cultural puppet. Do uniform definitions homogenize or specify? Do--Oish! Somebody stop me!

If the past knew so much that is right for today's use, why did their future - the "Now" as we know it - occur with all its warts and social maladies? A major fault with our recent ancestors' future is: We're it, FCOL. As Joan Rivers says, "Can we talk?" I think so, yes. We certainly have the words, but do we have the awareness. My question is, "Can we communicate?" Can we define our terms?

To say of emotion or intuition: "There are no words" does not mean that words may one day be developed. But rather that in emotion or intuition - there are no words...there are feelings. Each person has to experience a specific feeling event/emotion for himself/herself... to actively and personally define it. Can you show me how you define Love? Anger? Joy? Sadness?

The pollution of language is a serious threat to human relationship. As is the pollution of Nature a serious threat to our physical existence and life in general, as we know it. Any chance we'll "clean-up" our act? Our communications? Our chemistry? Our involvement?

Avoid substituting activity for involvement in your expressions. For example, don't ask a person to go to a movie or for a walk by the lake (activities) when what you want to do is spend time with him/her (involvement). Ask to spend time, then decide how...mutually. Ask for the involvement, then decide on the activity. Know what you seek. It takes a burden off the words.

Often it is we who betray the words, rather than the words that betray us. We try at times to cloak our feelings in words, then we curse the results. A crooked arrow rarely hits the target, I would venture.

Have you ever sat and stared at a closed book which is lying on a table? And wondered what it was in that book that made things happen in your mind? Wondered what thought was? Do words mean anything without experience? When you hear or read the word, "convention," e.g., does it mean anything to you if you've never experienced a convention? Or can you adequately define it from a dictionary? Is that the same thing? Experience vs. book definition: a fuller self-meaning is held by those with experience. What is a ball? Or a hod? Or love? Or relating? Or a convention?

There are objective words that have standing definitions which can be usefully passed along, generation to generation. Such words as tree, chair, rock, sky, food, road, etc. might fall into this basket. And there are other words that each of us have to define through aware-living. Such words as affection, grief, joy, happiness, etc. might be found in this basket. We have outer worldly words and inner personal words.   Be aware of the difference in definitional responsibility and usage. The other evening Anatole France whispered to me, "It is better to understand little than to misunderstand a lot."

Abstract conceptual terms, such as man, woman, life, forest, etc. are general constructs that hold no effect, they hold only description. To say man causes war or woman causes peace is meaningless for assigning specific do-age. Individuals do cause things, abstract terms cause nothing. You are not stopped by the forest. You are stopped by the big oak tree. Take care in using and in hearing words. Don't let your awareness be ambushed by versed verbalism. The legal profession, e.g., is based upon word usage and slippage. Laws are expressed in words by wordsmiths, and these "Ziploc" legal words are then managed and massaged in the marketplace [the courts] by degreed word merchants. Verbal obscurity is bred in "Legalese." The letter or the spirit of the law? That is the question, isn't it? In your personal and public efforts to create communicative-opportunity encourage your awareness to separate the tree(s) from the forest, the effective/affective from the descriptive, the verb(s) from the noun(s),... the spirit from the letter. Oh, and listen-up for those Mavens who would say, "Evermore" and even more.

Feelings are not easily put into words. It is a mismatch: there are no words (remember?). This is why so much poetry is obscure. The poet tries to write of things that are not carried well with words. Some poems strain so as to be trash. Obscure syntax does not necessarily reflect a subtle idea or a complex mind. Some arcane verses reveal nothing more than a cluttered mind expressing mush, at times of rather common-place things. Don't be impressed by obscurity, be impressed with clarity.

"Almost all the contents of the 'advanced' reviews are just 'Mary had a little lamb' translated into Hebrew and written in cipher." (Huxley) Do we have a problem?

"In the earlier times, the deep thinkers were the clear thinkers - Descartes, Spinoza, Locke, Leibniz. They knew exactly what they meant and said it. In the nineteenth century, some of the deeper thinkers among theologians and philosophers were muddled thinkers." (Whitehead) Yes, I believe we do... have a problem. No wonder we've been confused. We've been getting Seltzer-muck, and told, by the buttoned-down, zipped-up mavens, to applaud it. And bless our fear-filled, little selves we've been doing just that. But you don't need Huxley, or Whitehead, or Pogo to tell you when there's a rotten fish in your "educational 'fridge." You've got awareness. You've got soul. You've got heart. You can discern thick from thin, wheat from chaff, curd from whey, and "uff da" from fretten. So... bring on the context, and let's dance.

In communicating, words can not be precisely defined as they go from one person's tongue to another person's ear. How many spoken-words in a hundred do you think you actually hear? The cause behind the tongue is different than the cause behind the ear. Do you listen as quickly as you talk? The experiences are diverse, and the understandings may be close or far apart, depending upon the relationship and empathic skills of the people involved. Nothing can be related exactly. It suffers or gains in the translation and transition. There is rather a broad psychological-gap between people, however cozy or friendly we are.

Don't expect others to understand you perfectly, as you can not expect to understand them perfectly either. Work to move closer in understanding, but don't get "angry" at a miss,.. or "convention-al" at nearness.

Words in the dictionary are brief discussions about from-the-past terms invented to label gone-by events, sensations, etc. Just as some "work tools" nicely fit their purpose, some "word tools" are richly expressive because they were invented by masters in the area of involvement. Too often we, for example, come to view words as intellectual definitions, not as depictions of feeling awareness. Too often we view living as solely a one-dimensional episode, rather than as an expanding contextual awareness of our self-aspects in creating living. Those last two sentence were difficult to create, I hope they "fit their purpose" well... despite the limits of the printed word. Words can be just another "layer of boring" without the enthusiasm of interactive doing. What do you suppose "walk the talk" is all about? Be careful in assuming that "chatroom aerobics" keep you "socially fit." "Chatrooms," for the most part, were invented by "real nerds" to be used by "virtual loiterers."

Don't only look in dictionaries for the definitions of words, such as honesty, trust, truth, love, share, fear, living, relate, etc., but also look within self to see how you "actively define and create" words in your daily living. Be a verb, not a noun! Be a doer, not merely a by-stander. We each define life by our living of it, not only by someone else's written definitions in a book. Define your words, your living, through situational-awareness of your actions. Do living to help self more clearly sketch it, to make social choices, and to create a path with a heart. As Eenie, the oldest and head of the Way family, might have told Doc, the oldest and head of the Dwarf family, "Read your word-book, toil and mine the verbal gem-sources, and build your vocabulary-treasure. Hi-Ho and work your thinking wealth, so you can better pluck the pandered panache of pyritic pundits, however prettily adorned in emetic (pukey?) alliteration." Eenie Way,.. will you stop.

"I" messages about feelings and beliefs are a great idea, but they don't work well when you don't know how you feel or what you believe. Too usually, about most area of life, we depend upon what we've been taught to memorize (with about 90% memory loss). We spend little aware time creating/establishing effective personal principles, values, beliefs, and feelings as interactive social/ecological guideposts. "I" messages become an empty conversational-gimmick when used by a person who doesn't know self. Be aware of what you speak, as you speak. Living well is the result of aware adjustment during contextual activity. Lock-step, memorized preparation which dictates your "life" often precludes awareness. With the aware person, preparation is part of contextual awareness, not separate from it.

We live in a society of nouns, adjectives and adverbs (and expletives), not verbs. We're into codifying and embellishment, not action. Untested living shapes your opinions that skew too easily toward deception. Verbs express action and are readily checked-out. Adjectives and adverbs are often mercurial and fickle. Get in the game of creating verbs in your daily affairs, leave the noun-embellishment to the spectators.

In our search for understanding we have been known to define one unknown word (like self) with one or a cluster of equally vague word(s). Then we exclaim, "Now we've got it!" We use one, or more, misunderstood word(s) to define another misunderstood word. One thimble of actual understanding is worth three boxcars of confusing information.

And how about those every-day expressions that drop so easily off our tongues? Do we know what we're saying? Let's run through a few: Do your best, use something up, and falling in love...some common examples, right?

"Do your best!" Okay, but what does it mean? Does it mean - if in a race - run until you pass-out? If shooting a basketball, does it mean "make it" or "try to make it"? Which result is your best? Who decides?

"Who used up the toothpaste?" Does this mean "to take the last one (glob)"? As in: "Did you take the last cookie?" Did you use up the cookies? Actually the person who takes, or uses, the first piece, or amount, diminishes the stock by as much as does the last-piece taker. So who did use it up?

"Falling in love" is an expression to describe a lack of control. To fall is to have no protection or control against outcome. We do not fall into love. We fall "head over heels" in love. You may fall into a mudpuddle, but you fall in love...that's what I think it means. The awareness of meaning is critical to communicating. Taboos and hoorahs are all a matter of social interpretation. Communication is an area of wide use, immense clutter.

Culture has influence in every nook, a finger in every pie. A sneeze is not sneezed the same in different languages. Can you believe that? Sneeze pronunciations (noises) vary across cultures (according to L. M. Boyd, Sacramento Bee newspaper, 12/7/78): English - Atchoo; Chinese - Hah-chee; French - Atchoum; Russian - Apchi; Finnish - Atshi; Czech - Herpche; Indonesian - Bersin; Japanese - Kushan.... Get outa' here...anybody ever heard an Eskimo sneeze? Who records this stuff?

Laughter is also different around the world. How natural is natural? It makes a person wonder, huh? How much of what we do is learned? How much can we unlearn, if we have the will and awareness? How much can you alter the mold? Indeed, how high and wide is your piece of sky? What is your best?

"If you pick at a sore, it'll never get better" is an expression that comes to mind whenever I hear gossip coming from my mouth or anyone else's mouth. Gossip always seems to be picking at scabs. I can't think of a single case of gossip that was up to any good.

What do you think: Is gossip a useful social tool; the first stage of honest inquiry about how others live? Or is gossip like a snake, having no friends or allies? As for me, I don't see a gram of social worth in gossip; I don't care to pet it or pass it on or listen to it. My word-book tells me that "gossip" comes from "godsib", or God-related. Egad, have we come that far,.. really?

People who are addicted to gossip for their intellectual-fuel are inept about creating ideas or being productively active in living. Gossip is a deep rut, set in the past, in which all memory is fiction. Gossips seem to believe that the act of getting their tongues and lips to move together is a high art-form--but without rumors and idle-chatter about others they run empty quickly. This huge need for fuel may explain why we make nine-minute heroes and heroines of so many odd-posturing entertainers and celebrities. A gossipy tongue, or pen, is only as guilty as the gossipy ears and eyes that devour the grist. Hearing or reading gossip, like second-hand smoke, is not good for you. To be a gossip-addict falls into the "deep-sick" range of self no-no.

Most of us are pretty good at "smelling" gossip when we hear it, or speak it. But, quite often, we miss identifying it when we <u>think</u> gossip. A lot of our time is wasted in thinking gossip. How much of the information that we get from friends, colleagues, or the media is gossip? How about that obscene or racist "joke", or that biased, opinionated political-column? Nothing good comes from hearing, reading, speaking, laughing at, or thinking gossip. When you grow up, you can give it up. I'll tell you what--Let's give it up together.

Comments regarding another person's character, motives, behaviors, weaknesses, strengths, etc., are most meaningful when made directly to that person. All negative stuff, and possibly some of the positive stuff, is gossip. Let me ask you: is harboring unexpressed ill-feelings, dislikes, envy, jealousy, prejudice, etc., a form of gossip? Can it negatively influence your conduct and comments regarding a person(s)? Can such opinions hold you captive? Can such opinions damage your social-health?

"You can know a person by what he/she says of others" is a saying I find instructive. When you hear a person judge someone (either as good or bad), you can learn much of the speaker, for he/she uses words that are clues of himself/herself. Measure your judgments with care, and see what you learn about self from your words of others, or Nature.

"I hate to throw stones at departed heroes, or those not present... but.." is the lead-in of a snide coward. Such remarks are a poison to both the tongue that speaks them and the ears that embrace them. Where do you draw-the-line on gossip, and when do you start drawing it? Can we handle awareness? When do we say, "Stop!" to self and to others? Is awareness "user friendly"?

Are you interested in wasting your time and energy? It's simple to do: just stir the mud-of-gossip with your organ (oar-gan?) of choice. Be it your eyes, ears, nose, or throat, your mind or pen...be it a wink, a crinkle, a twinkle, a blink, a word, a shrug, or a nod, actively or passively. Gossip is a negative flow against your social-investment, in every case. Are you still wondering what my position on gossip is? Is it all right to gossip about gossip? How about weeds? What's your slant on weeds?

Now that you're warmed-up, either running with me or against me, let's take a quick glance at lying. One thing that I dislike about lying, as a communicative art-form, is that most lies keep the liar focused in the past. Most of my lies have a home in the past. I'll exaggerate the future, but I'll lie about the past. A past-lie occurs when an effort to alter facts is a-tongue. Facts, as well as I can tell, always belong to the past - it's dreams that belong to the future. We don't get too torqued with someone's "dream-stretching", but "fact-massages" often put a sour look on our faces. We'll freely tease (accuse) a person of "lying" about their future intentions, but in fairness, a lie is not a lie until it comes to rest in the past. Inaccurate tales of the future are called exaggerations; inaccurate tales of the past, lies.

Lies, as you know, can be in words or actions. I suppose that some of the really top liars can lie in their thoughts and emotions, as well. The "lie" can be as blunt as a brick in the face, or it can be subtle, even seductive and cute. For example, a person primps and dresses neatly and precisely, leaving behind a house that is a pit of trash and garbage. The lie is: "What others don't see, isn't me." Lying is socially destructive and has been a top-ten item on the "How to make enemies and antagonize people" list since it appeared in the first "Garden of Eden" newsletter. When you cheat or steal, in any form or degree, you are a liar, and others will feel unsafe with you. How about a spiritual lie? Can the spirit lie? I'm asking your take on that. Any opinion, impression, sense on this question? Oh, and what's Mother Nature's rule on lies?

A final comment about lying: lying is a great way to communicate if you want people to decide that they don't want anything to do with you. That's it... for lying. To tell the truth, I'm glad that's over, aren't you? Can you imagine a whole chapter on lying? I'd be all negative and wrinkled before I got through three foul-pages. My name is Mike and I'm a ___.

Listening and Silence

The interested, aware listener is never out of his/her element. The aware listener can easily glide through social levels with comfort and fun. Listening is being aware. Listen to self, listen to others, listen to Nature. The good listener is rarely lonely.

Just because a person doesn't say much, doesn't make him/her a good listener. Being distant and aloof is, likewise, not necessarily a clue to a good listener. Some people are silent in order to listen, to observe, to learn of/from self, others, or Nature. There is also the "cleverly" silent person who has heard that silence indicates an intellectual depth and pensive mystery-of-personality (which he/she does not possess, but wishes others to attribute to him/her). This is a "deceptive" silence. This person is silent to avoid revealing to others his/her true shallows of character or narrowness of purpose.

Never bet that silence is an indication of anything other than silence. Don't assume that silence means good ideas, profound thoughts, depth of character, or intense listening. Silence may indicate desirable relating traits but it doesn't guarantee them. Don't be fooled by clear eyes - they could be backed up by an empty mind. How are the amps in your lamps?

Listening, for the aware person, can be an active contact sport, a debate, a wading into the environment and stimulus-fields of exchange. Listening does not necessarily mean being silent or mute. I've known some stonily silent people who manage nicely - thank you - to avoid listening to a word that anyone says. Our classrooms, churches, and political fora (or forums, if you please) are crowded with poor listeners. I remember a fellow at college; he would look attentively at the teacher then jot words on a paper. A good listener, a good student? No, he was a fake. He wrote letters to his friends of his feigned sexual-feats, and letters to his family of his feigned academic-feats. He flunked-out,.. but at least he wrote letters. Good listening is not a lazy activity - it takes energy.

Much of what we pass-off as the give-and-take of conversation is habit and reflex: not much awareness in either one. Is anybody in your circle really listening? Are you?

Questions and Answers

To be aware of them, is to be.

"We can make our lives sublime,
And, departing, leave behind us
Footprints on the sands of time;
Footprints, that perhaps another
Sailing o'er life's solemn main,

A forlorn and shipwrecked brother,
Seeing, shall take heart again."
(Longfellow)

Q. How can a person do this?
A. By actively producing questions and answers in the pursuit of creating opportunity (relating) and social value (sharing).

We are taught early in our lives to ask other

people's questions and to accept other people's answers. We call this school. When you ask old questions for old reasons you will accept old answers as correct, even when they no longer fit. We are wired early with certain question formats, for which the teacher has the answer book. When the format is: non-creative in, non-creative out, we seek and accept pre-packaged answers. What do children learn through the questions and answers that adults use with them, and through the questions and answers that adults encourage from them? What do adults learn with their own and from their children's Q&A patterns?

Most often we have been taught to view "answer" as having some absolute property; and that once we have an "answer" we move beyond the "question." Because answers follow questions, right? It's a natural progression, right? Most questions aired in classrooms are requests for pre-determined, past-discovered information. Thus as students we come to view and think of living in terms of a right vs wrong model of information. Give a wrong answer, the kids laugh; give a right answer, the teacher smiles.

Some schools, homes, churches attempt to teach children by having them memorize set questions and set answers. This is called catechizing. Some people try to use this same method in learning how to live life. They like to believe that set-questions and set-answers exist for effective living. Such learning by rote creates fear when events occur for which pre-set answers have not been taught. Myths are made of such stuff in our "yupped-up" Republic as we fearfully search for a personal guru, or "shrink," or whatever, to find set-answers to set-questions. In such a dodge from a creative ideal, we get caught in the warp of a strange contradiction: free prisoners.

What are we seeking to teach our children? Do we know? What virtues, traits, etc., are needed in tomorrow's adults? Do we know? We seem to favor "smart" children - the ones with the memorized "right" answers that match the pre-set test questions - above all others. But what sort of a society will evolve when all the control positions are filled by programmed "smart" people? Will "smart" conquer all? Don't future generations need any other virtues in stock? For example, is Economic Mastery all that everyone will need to know the questions and answers to? I find myself doubting that. But in case I'm wrong, and should live so long... do you have any old tests that I can use?

Students need to practice at home and rehearse at/in school, those creative, cooperative skills that will serve them well, when they perform as adults. We have to overcome our high-tech intoxication and accept that most areas of everyday living do not have rigid, pre-set Q's & A's. There are few 1+1=2 equations in relating and sharing.

Our students, at increasingly younger ages (look at the Japanese test-stress and our early grades SAT-diet) seek the "Fountain of Answers." Questions of intellectual inquiry don't get a student into college, set answers do. There is little reward for the student who only memorizes good questions. Students, being no dummies, put their energy into piling-up answers. But rote answers don't give a student practice in "impossible" curiosity: questions based on creative awareness do. "Cheat-sheets", you may recall, are lists of answers, not lists of clever, exploratory questions. I've never heard anyone call a "cheat-sheet" interesting. Are there "multiple questions" tests?.. in school?... There are in living. There are in humor,.. drama,...

Is the small child who darts in front of your car an inquiry or a lecture, a question or an answer? Does the clock on the wall ask a question or give an answer? A burning building with you on the 10th floor, or a spring breeze on your cheek: questions or answers? A person must be judged by both his/her questions and his/her answers; the flexibility and creative range of his/her total context. Memory without creative imagination is neither an answer, nor a question. It's information stored without a hope of being invited to the "power party." Does a reflex-effect give a person access? Do questions and answers exist outside the cortical context of self, others and Nature. Are these good Q's, bad A's, or bad vice, good versa? Our Q's & A's are a broad window to self. How about that fly in your soup--is it a Q, an A, or an "impossible" curiosity? Or that soup on your "fly"?

So what do our questions and answers teach our children? Antoine de Saint-Exupery, in The Little Prince, said: "Grown-ups love figures. When you tell them you have a new friend, they never ask you any questions about essential (individual) matters. They never say to you, 'What does his voice sound like? What games does he love best? Does he collect butterflies?' Instead they demand, 'How old is he? How much does he weigh? How much money does his father make?' Only from these figures do they think they have learned anything about him."

What, in fact, do such questions tell Exupery's grown-ups? What do such practices teach our children about addressing life and getting to the substance unique to the matter of interest? In his The Book: On the Taboo Against Knowing Who You Are, Alan Watts gave a potentially useful hint when he said, "Problems that remain persistently insoluble should always be suspected as questions asked in the wrong way, like the problem of cause and effect. Make a spurious division of one process into two, forget that you have done it, and then puzzle for centuries as to how the two get together."

Do questions shape the answers? Do good answers proceed from good questions? Do Q's always precede A's? Is it a natural law that Q's always take precedence of A's? How about the waggish exchange over: "Jesus is the Answer." to which someone posed: "What is the Question?"?

Is there, do you believe, any truth in the notion that answers are just questions that are flipped and turned inside our minds? If so, then by more clearly understanding our questions we should more readily grasp the answer when it appears. If the answer dwells within the question, then too the question resides in the answer. Does this idea help my Q and A awareness any?

Is the Q, or is the A more important? Are related Q's and A's, in fact, separate?

In theory-building the question posed certainly tends to dictate (contain) the answer. Much research is critically accused of supporting a pre-conceived answer rather than testing the question. The question often, as posed, drags us to a desired answer. Mutual silence may be the only question that does not hold its own answer, for such silence has two sides: yours and mine... and the twain are mute, in this case. And you know what has been said about "the twain."

Can a person ask a question using more than the words and information he/she has available? When someone asks a question is he/she airing a bias, or seeking new information? Is it possible for the person-in-the-street to have sufficient awareness to ask informed, constructive questions and to recognize useful answers? Is it possible to cut through the "Spam?" Of course, it is. Awareness, imagination, and intuition are marvelous "Spam" dicers.

So, why all the words about this "Hound and Fox" Q and A stuff? Simply because, to better come to "know self" is our "pursuit-of-the-day life-time-menu item." Your questions indicate your theory and data base regarding a topic, and these same self-factors dictate what you will accept as an answer. You can better come to "know self" by being aware of your theories and biases through their influence upon your questions and the answers you accept, as meaningful. A question without an in-context theory, or bias is idle, and no "meaningful" answer is possible. At the very least, a person has "gotta' have heart,"... if "attitude decoding" is an item of personal-interest.

To assume that we all have the same definition of terms...however common the terms...is a conversational-abyss into which many a grand subject has plunged to an early demise. Historically, many a budding relationship has entangled and languished in a smothering definitional-tar-pit. To avoid conversational-feebleness, Voltaire, I believe, would advise, "When you speak to me, define your terms."

It is almost impossible for two people to arrive at "common grounds," when they have done a poor job in establishing their terms. If you attempt to reply to a question without first clarifying the term-points, you may be, unawarely, conceding some essential assumption(s). Your verbal guide-posts will turn into a mishmash of tacky-taffy, rather than into mutual understanding.

For example, if someone asks, "Do you believe in God?" Since they didn't say a God, it seems likely that they have a definition of God already in hand. Ask them to explain what they understand God to be. This is not an attempt to split hairs, but a sincere effort to understand their assumptions and therefore give them a better answer. The Q and A exchange effectiveness is directly proportional to the joint level of available awareness: low awareness, low outcome; high awareness, high outcome.

William James, noted philosopher/psychologist, said, "Any question can be made immaterial by subsuming all its answers under a common head." For example, a Shah of ancient Persia declined to attend the horse races by stating, "It is already known to me that one horse can run faster than another." He makes the question "which horse" immaterial.

And a campaigning Abe Lincoln, when asked by a heckler "Do you believe that the slaves should be free?" pulled the plug on the question's anger by stating, "I believe in (our constitutional form of) democracy." Abe went back to basics.

In most conversation we prefer to engage in areas and topics where we feel safe or superior. This leads to a lot of "trivia spooning" and informational one-(or-two)ups-manship. Those questions that surface in discussional exchanges, despite their innocent faces, are usually asked with some answer in mind. So, in replying, when you do anything besides agree (in degree) or disagree (in degree) with others you will be classed as odd, at best. We all seem to enjoy operating under the sanction: "It's always easier for me to remember my questions and my answers, than for me to remember your questions and your answers." Participants in a debate learn little from their opponents when they totally distract themselves with their own position.

People of all ages, in disappointingly high numbers, have been found to be more aware of their own hair, which they absently search for split ends, than they are of your side of the discussion. In fact, some people only ask answers - they may put their words in the form of a question, even to include the "?" mark but they're asking answers. When you go along with their biased Q & A shoves, you give-up the chance even to be wrong. These slanted exchanges place you, on your hands and knees, in the hazardous "fast lane" of a buffalo herd. Felt stepped-on lately?

As we near the end of our Q & A section, let me suggest that you avoid trying to give a complete (or perfect) answer to an incomplete, poor question. For example, "What do you think of me?" he/she asks. Could he/she be asking you an "answer" here? In what context is he/she asking you? As an old friend, as a fellow flier on a flight to Japan, at a job interview, as a lover, as a driver, as a cook, as a short person, as an etc.? Context alert! Until you determine the context of his/her question, don't cater to answer.

"There is no direct answer to an irrational question which is why one Zen master replied (to such a question), 'When you know the answer you won't ask the question.'" (Alan Watts, Psycho Therapy East and West, p. 147.) Since most of us are not yet full-minded Zen masters, let's strive to reduce our irrational questions and not encourage any from our associates. That a person has a thousand good answers does not assure that he/she has one good question. Don't be seduced-by or cower-to rank, prestige, charm, or anger - let your self-awareness be the balance weight of your Q & A common-sense. Don't be fear-filled by any Q or any A, whether invented by you, or others... or even those offered, or thrust upon, you by Nature.

Questions and answers are important girders in building the bridge for spanning the "psychological gap" that exists between Self, Others, and Nature. How effective your questions and how useful your answers in daily context creation depend upon how much freedom your parents, et. al., as teachers were courageous enough to entrust to you during your early days. Just watch the creative questions that a toddler "asks" as he/she checks out the world, circles a tree, picks up a bug, looks at a star. Encourage your child to ask good questions by aiding him/her to enjoy success in his/her ramblings. Children learn something through pain and failure (examples often of un-aware questions), but they learn <u>much more</u> through success. Be a courageous teacher. Be a courageous student. Trust self, and you will more ably trust and entrust others.

Communicating is not just a guy-thing or just a girl-thing, it's a people-thing. As a species we have a unique and marvelous ability. Why waste it? (This is a question, not an answer.) Never consider a question as closed, nor an answer as final. This range of responsibility-flexibility is not meant for small children, or the creatively faint of heart. Our ability to communicate is a responsibility to be shared. Work on your word skills, your Q & A skills, your communication skills, your creating "a life" skills.

Some closing thoughts on the communication mudslide:

Some things are better said in music than in words. Music can set the mood. When there are no words, try silence. When there are no songs, try humming from the heart.

"Words are wise men's counters, without value of their own; they are the money only of fools and politicians." (Will Durant)

"Language is the greatest invention. All education comes from language," some say. Language is a social tool... both marvelous and mischievous in potential.

"Learn a new language and get a new soul" (Czech proverb). This says well that language expands the person; giving one a larger view of living with others. Expand your own language, native and foreign, poetic and prosaic, to expand your thoughts.

Language is also a social event. Children do not learn language in isolation. Children learn language through social interactive-awareness. Isolation does not encourage language exchange, nor does noise.

"The amount of noise which anyone can bear undisturbed stands in inverse proportion to his mental capacity." (Schopenhauer) Did the man say that noise tortures intellect? How about noise and my golf game? Now that mix is an assassination,.. pure and brutal. I'm most fond of golf carts, weed whackers, and leave blowers,.. and low flying aircraft are also fun.

Are some people attempting to get words to speak louder than actions? Our politicians are certainly getting a lot of practice - ouch! - in that "litter-box."

A 'phone answering machine (with no messages) lets you know when nobody cared enough to call. The big zero says it all... about your communications-diet.

In the application of words, it is said: "Strength takes care of itself; we defend our weakness."

A major value of listening with active awareness is that it allows the speaker to share in the listener's energy. Both parties gain. Are we <u>awarely</u> listening to each other? Have you heard from Nature lately? Did you listen, awarely?

Secrets and gossip are the language of the lonely.

The excuse of a poor memory is viewed by some people as a cardinal virtue (e.g., witnesses at congressional investigative-hearings). They seem to be telling us: "If I can't remember where I've come from, how can you expect me to know that I'm lost."

The most complete term, in our language, marking a person's passage in life is: Died. The unavoidable verb. An itty-bitty verb, or two, sneak into everyone's life... sooner or later. Be active, be aware, be ready.

"The ancient Goths of Germany...had all of them a wise custom of debating everything of importance to their state twice; that is, - once drunk, and once sober: - Drunk - that their counsels might not want vigor; - and Sober - that they might not want discretion." (From Laurence Sterne's <u>Tristram Shandy</u>, p. 355) So it's <u>vigorous</u> <u>discretion</u> we seek, is it?

"If you want to know someone's faults, praise him to his peers. They'll set you straight." (Ben Franklin)

The honored prophet is the one who sets his/her prophesies so far in the future that he/she is long dead before they <u>don't</u> come true. Who honors the weather forecaster - too easy to check him/her out. Go for the year 2840 a.d. "On October 3, 2840, the weather will be...."

The shoulder shrug may be our most meaningful social gesture.

"Everything has been said," is an accurate old quote, until you think of something new to say. Don't give-up talking until you give-up thinking. It hasn't all been done yet... you're here.

"The flea on the tip-end of the lion's tail is the last to learn that the lion has died." Information pales as you near the extremes of a system or organization. The tip-end flea is a warped analogy, but it's cute.

Seek to have around you those who think, explore and create, and not merely parrot thoughtlessly words from books. No one needs any help in being ignorant.

Sarcasm is the lowest form of ridicule. To be sarcastic is to try to hurt someone with words...and to be cute about it. It's not becoming.

Mouth control: substitute a nice word for a negative word. For example, princess for pig...(without sarcasm).

"The history of the development of language...is a history of the progressive analysis of ideas." (Whitehead)

Conversation is, for the most part, an exercise of "interruptions and trivialities." (Durant)

There is no such thing as the "unvarnished truth." All information comes slanted by a point of view, "varnished" that is. There aren't any "unvarnished lies" either. "Gossip, anyone?"

Much of what I used to see as aloofness in people I have come to learn is fear. Fear cuts deep into our social practice-time.

When someone we like tells us they like us (love us) we are willing to accept them at their word without too much investigation into their sanity. Yet, later when that same person "turns their terms" (they don't like or love us any longer) we interrogate them and attack their position as neurotic, question their honesty and their sanity. We find them both blind and crazy usually. We tend to be sweet to positive input, and sour to negative.

Abuse and rudeness. We excuse a great deal of angry, irrational, hurtful behavior with the word "love." It's not "love" at the base of all this selfish, petty, lashing-out crap. Fear, not love, is the fuel of anger and hatred. Is there, perhaps, a trace of Genetic Self in these words?

People yell at each other, at their children, at strangers and they call it talking. The words drown in the emotions.

Anger is the voice of fear. Have you heard it lately?

"Humpty-Dumpty anger" - that's when a person absolutely comes apart, explodes. They anger over nothing that is apparent to you. The trigger is an internal stress-load. They explode all over you. It's like being "sucker punched" in a bar as you mind your own business. It's not fun. Why do they punch you? Because you're there? Or because you're their___?

Some people act as if any comment or gesture, or even silence at times, by others is a line in the dirt over which to argue. When the anger becomes "thick over thin issues" and "push comes to punch over a gnat" you are waltzing with a "neurotic out-of-controller." Excuse yourself - mid-sentence if possible - remove your jugular from their grip and scat-scram (or whichever "juke" works most quickly). Pack-up all your "there and their" and do a "fly-pattern."

When dealing with a chronic abuser, drinker, sick-o, etc., we wrongly think we need to make things "right" for them. Many a professional and amateur therapist get sucked into this role of attending to the chronic-part of the person, the well-rehearsed part. Don't waste your energy trying to make a "chronic" feel comfortable about being chronic. Don't deal with their social weaknesses. See if they have some social strengths to build on. They've got their social weaknesses polished to a fine edge. Absolutely perfect for turning your "kindness of heart" into tomorrow's confetti.

With some people you can feel lonely when you spend time with them. The more time, the more lonely.

Avoid living little lies. It's practice for living "whoppers" when the stress goes up or the levee breaks.

Say what you mean, if you know what you mean. Words are best used to inform, not to impress. Actions are better impressors.

When someone says: "I want you" (forever of course), they might better say: "Can I borrow you for a minute?' You might ask, "Can we define terms here?"

As I come to know self more fully, I find some discussions and attempted exchanges are not to my comfort or interest. I avoid these snags as cordially as I am able or permitted to do so. I refuse to swim in a cesspool, even though I like to swim.

"I can't understand my son. He won't listen to me," a parent lamented. "To understand another person you must listen to him/her," goes the adage. How might a parent teach a child to listen? By modeling it; listen to your child. Could this be one meaning for "what goes around, comes around"?

We spend a lot of our time speaking, listening, watching, reading, or writing. In school we have classes to practice reading, writing, and speaking skills; but is there any training in watching? Are there any classes in listening? By the way, you control your rate of speaking, right? Who controls your rate of listening? How fast can you listen? How fast can you watch?

When someone speaks you can: 1) ignore them, 2) pretend to listen, 3) selectively listen, 4) attentively listen, 5) empathically listen (active awareness with the intent to understand self and others), 6) study your hair for split-ends, or 7) pick your nose (passively or actively).

It is said:

10% of communications is in the words we say.
30% of communications is in our sounds/inflections.
60% of communications is in our body language.

What sort of body-language vocabulary do you use? Boy, at 60% usage impact, it's worth being aware of. You may be absolutely "trashing" me, right now.

To understand - listen with ears, eyes, and "heart." Listen for feeling as well as for words, gestures, and inflections. "An attitude," even of deep silence, will shout loudly at your "heart."

Psychological-space is given to others through understanding and respect (acceptance and recognition). When the physical-air is taken from a person, that person loses interest in everything else <u>but</u> getting air. The same is true with psychological-space. When all understanding and respect is shut-off, others will lose interest in relating to you...as you will also lose interest in relating to them. Everyone will be gasping for psychological-air... whoops, psychological-<u>space</u>.

Touching is an important and effective way to communicate. But the harder the touch the cruder the message. Touching sends signals across the physical-space between us - keep it gentle.

Avoid giving advice. Say what you sense or observe, if you must...or if asked, but otherwise let the person concerned take their own counsel. You can tell someone what <u>you</u> would do, but don't tell them what <u>they</u> should do. I'm working on this one.

In the early stages of dating, couples chatter amicably about all manner of trivia, such as popcorn, TV., beer, cars, a cat on a fence; some even dabble in current events. This chatter gets its heat from passion's flame. When the flame dies, the heat dies...and silence's chill becomes a dulling guest.

Being around most married couples is like living on the San Andreas Fault - the big quake may come at any moment.

And finally: Don't try to make sense out of non-sense. It'll blow your kite right out of the sky. Keep that kite in the air, pal! Be actively aware - **LISTEN!** Oh, and don't try to whistle while you burp. Systems-overloads can get messy. Do you have any Q's? Do you have any A's?

What is the Purpose of Sex?

Is sex your servant or your master? Is the human body a temple or a playground? Are you a fine tapestry, or a tattered door-mat?

"The beginning of understanding is the recognition that sex is not primarily something we do, but something we are." (Rev. Kenneth Greet) And sexual intercourse is not simple-recreation provided by Nature to erase our boredom, but it is an avenue for self expression and awareness. Is Rev. Greet talking Gender, only? Some among us believe that sex without intercourse is a lamp without a glow, a hook without bait. What's your slant on sex?

Each of us believe that what we do with our personal sexual attitude and behavior are correct. About others we're not so generous. Except, of course, when they're "hitting" on us, and we think it's a turn-on... A "cool choice." When things go bump in the night, it's the physical-self that calls out, "Meow!" Freud named that cat "Id." A randy force that needs taming is ol' Id... advised Freud.

Sexual intercourse is a social event when performed by consenting human adults, and a relating event of sharing when done by mature humans. Consensual social events are "games." All games have rules. Sex, as consensual social behavior, has rules. Rape is an anti-social event of selfish aggression. Rape breaks the rules... but then, rape is <u>not</u> consensual. Rape sows the seed for chaos.

It is easy to understand how passion (mislabeled Love) can turn to passion (aggression) called Hate. But love is never the opposite side of hate. It is not love that turns to hate, it is passion recycled or warped that you are experiencing.

We all say that we seek love, yet we all too quickly settle for passion's temporary embrace. We pass by the classroom offering mature, long-term love in the short-term interest of heeding the quickened, quirky pulse of passion.

Do we feel that sex is love because only during moments of sexual passion do most of us sense any generosity toward another person? Can this be?

When someone says to you, "I love you," is that good, or is it bad, for you? For them? Who started this expression, this concept? Is there really such a bridge between humans? What do the words "I love you" represent? What is this encircling feeling that we label as love? Is it a sense of security? A rush of passion? I'm in the hunt for self-awareness here. Can you hear the hounds?

Is there some reason that we say "we practice sex," as in "to practice safe sex"? Is this simply a word choice, or does it say something about human sexual behavior? Do other animals <u>practice</u> sex? Other organisms have forms of sexual intercourse; do any, likewise, have a sound, a grunt, a moo-tone, a canted-wink for expressing "love"?

A lack of awareness is a major difficulty in living. Awareness in the self-aspects within our living-context (personal, professional, interpersonal, natural, etc.) is critical to a good outcome. We are often fooled by "sex" because of a heightened sensuality "glow" which blinds our awareness. We like to think we are "aware" when we ride in passion's carriage. We like to believe that we know exactly what we are doing and why we say, "I love you." But during sexual intercourse as sensation increases, awareness can decrease. Being aware is not the same as being alert. Alertness is basic to external responsiveness. Awareness is basic to internal "pre-sponsiveness." You can be alert without being aware, but you cannot be aware without being alert. Blurry choice-points are common during "horny" episodes. The galloping carriage of passion is a familiar visitor with the potholes and ditches of life's "rut."

In the Sixties when sex became a popular religion in America, its flame roared high. The big dream was to have a body without a mind, to have time without a future. Sex was to be a religion without a future and its language a French kiss. With one-night-stands as its benediction, venereal diseases became its curse. The social result: crowded streets and lonely people. Its motto:

> When money rules, marry richly.
> When knowledge rules, marry wisely.
> When sex rules, do not marry.

Sex is not meant to be entertainment, an anxiety reducer, mutual masturbation, or a sleep inducer. However, sex is a grounding event. When "having sex" we, each of us, feel, for just a moment perhaps, that we understand something special about life. The Ground Zero of life, during sex, is seen as simple and pure -- and we all cherish this moment of simplicity in the firestorm reality we call our daily life. We could stay forever. Some of us try to. Is that a canted wink gracing your "glow?"

Money has long defined our working relationships, to our endless disappointment. Are we going to let sex define our interpersonal relationships, to our total destruction? Is sex your goal in life? Or is enduring relationship your goal?

Sex can be as enchanting and delicate as watching a butterfly on a warm spring day embrace a flower...or sex can be as blunt and dulling as running at full speed into a tree. But remember many a horny person can find sweeping beauty even in an insult, or deep pain.

An old fellow once told me, "Young men just out of puberty's monastery have given sex a leadership role in their lives. But sex is not a leader; it has no vision and it has no memory." A limit of the genitals, once they become interested in mingling, you may have noticed, is they do not ask questions. That same fellow claimed, "Awareless sex places us too near the edge of free-fall into chaos." Of course, he might have been wrong.

Regardless of how reserved and proper a person pretends to be, sex can, at times, force itself as the main course, not merely as a discrete dessert. The on-going "serve and volley" question for social-thinkers is: "Is sex in its butt-naked full-range a social A-bomb or a cap-pistol?"

How can a person have sex without acting like an animal? I don't think you can (unless you're British, maybe) for sex is a pure and natural act. Sex is animal. If you do sex, you do animal. Why deny our nature? Why try to make sex something other than it is? But you don't have to bark at the moon in doing it. Even if we act like animals, we don't have to think like them. You can at least sign the dance card with your _real_ name.

Graffiti: "Sex would be all right, if you just didn't have to touch."

We show the shallowness of our thinking and of our value-base when we refer to sexual intercourse as "having gone all the way" in a relationship. All the way to where?

A sign of maturity is not being less aware of sex, but that you are equally aware of what you share after sex. Is he as funny-witty _after_ sex; she, as charming-alluring?

Many males are afraid of sex, because it controls and dominates their thoughts, directions, energies, and goals as mysteriously as a magnet controls iron filings. Iron filings do not know where, when, why, or how they'll end up. So too it is with many males and sex's appetite. Praying in church one minute, barking at the moon the next; very disconcerting for those who would be bishops.

"We've made LOVE into a three-letter word: SEX."

With some, one great advantage in aging is: they don't permit passion to blur their view of the full character of the opposite sex in meeting. But some of us seem to remain the foolish slaves to passion's veil forever. Personally, I am not in the least concerned about sex in my eighties, but I am interested in sharing Relationship in all my decades, however many they may be. Sex is invited, but not necessary to pluck the weeds of my boredom. I'll leave that chore to love. It's a grand age you are when you can laugh at sex's blind command.

Without love our ambition -- our joy -- in living falls off our Tree of Knowledge and drops to the earth like a withered leaf, there to turn to dust. A life without love is the pit of pessimism. Without love we are cowards; without sharing we are alone; without relationship we are lost without definition, awareness, or social purpose in living. Love-relationship is more than the contact of skin on skin.

With sex, we all feel, "I can do that," but mention "relate" and "share" and we "go into the fetal position" of incompetence. When we're out there "sexing" with someone, we wax poetic of "relating," crack wise of "sharing." Tall buildings aren't so hard to leap, when camping on Fantasy Island, huh?

If you believe that politics make strange bedfellows, have you taken a look at what sex does? Actually, strange becomes a high level compliment when dealing in the parameters of political and sexual adventures.

We humans are a herd animal. But we have softened our rutting war: every male privately can believe he is a stallion, or the main bull on campus since our sexual activity is now socially selective and involves less head-butting. With humans the sexual act is one in which more males participate -- due to the concept of monogamy (which is unherd-like behavior). We males, and females, too, get swept up by sexual prowess problems; sex becomes defined by performance concerns. We find that, socially, we try to be something which we are not, physically. When we actually <u>learn</u> new, to us, sexual-behavior ideas from the sexual-technique books or XXX-rated films, we should give serious thought to whether such behavior fits us... in character and personality.

We have confused ourselves with the constant emphasis on sex and the silly idea that the sex-drive "norm" is that of an anxiety-ridden pornomaniac. Many people have come to think they have sexual problems if they have less than a mythical, insatiable sex drive. Market "wisdom" says, "Sex sells. And Big-Lie-Sex sells BIG." The market is interested in your consumption, not in your satisfaction, sanity, or self-awareness.

Quite frankly, humans have not known what to do socially about sex for some time now. We have heard social scholars speak of sublimating it, freeing it, condemning it, censoring it, flaunting it, exploiting it, caressing it, selling it, improving it, forbidding it, taxing it (God forbid! They wouldn't!) We all have the tools (or are they toys, as Lawrence avers?) for sex, and therefore most of us are bound to dabble with it (sex) sooner or later, for better or worse. What shall we do with this burden? this pleasure? this "thing," of which we all have one?

We have nearly succeeded in turning sex into an action; rather than something of broader context-meaning. By making it only an action, sex becomes something else we humans can deny ourselves, and another sin is created. We try to push sex into a category outside of our nature. Now we are not sure how to <u>be</u> male or female (sex) -- we try to "act" sex. We concern ourselves with orgasms, positions, endurance, potency, closets, etc., and divorce ourselves from <u>our sex.</u> How little faith we have in what we are and in what we can become. Progressive social-creation cannot afford that we spend all of our time either above or below the navel, internally or externally. It is an issue of attitude, not an issue of our nature, that renders some people sexless to us in our feelings toward them. The sex drive is a strong enough force to cause two people to couple, but it is never a strong enough force to <u>keep</u> people coupled. The men who overemphasize sex and the women who encourage this attitude seek relationship as a part of sex, rather than finding sex as a pleasant part of a relationship.

Having sex, however intensely or energetically, and making love, (sharing in creating the moment through the behavior of sex) are not the same. We deceive ourselves harshly by saying we "made love," if in fact we merely "had sex." This barren deception is the desert in which the concept of Mutual Masturbation roves. The land where $1 + 1 = \underline{nada}$.

Too often people have sex, in a spasm of sequential frenzy, to exhaust an appetite, not to build relationship. When we do not deny to ourselves the faintest urge to sexual intercourse, soon no urge for the current partner remains. So we begin the search once again for a fresh urge in the form of a new mate. We damn the shortcomings of such immature encounters, but we rarely cancel the direction. In such "eating frenzies" people do not "relate and share" love, they "consume" sex. Fear's nickname is "Carnal."

Carnal knowledge does not guarantee carnal joy or carnal understanding. People who march solely to the drum of their appetites do so with a narrow motive: they are users. Sex with such people is neurotic angst behavior, or worse. What they present as enthusiasm and interest is selfish desperation. A trait which they explain away as yet another "uncontrollable addiction" of theirs. If you enjoy being a "fix" for someone's cravings, good luck. Being "yesterday's leftovers" is not my idea of fun. Addictions blur context. Do you choose to be the "blur of someone's neurotic eye"?

Nelson Algren in his "Three Rules for a Good Life" told us about this potential glitch in his third rule: Never go to bed with anybody who has more troubles than you do. The quicker you dive into bed with a thinly known acquaintance or a stranger, the greater your chances for violating rule #3 and gaffing the good life. This rule assumes, of course, that you enjoy a reasonable state of mental health, and at least a half cup of discretion.

A closing thought:

Sex is but one small room in the mansion of Relationship. It is a room that once its door is open, permitting one to visit there as one chooses, it adds comfort to the rest of the house. But the sex-room is not the whole of it, and it is too small a room for continuous dwelling. When this room is left closed or unvisited it can create severe distractions from the joys to be shared in the other rooms. We turn sex into a struggle by seeing it as the only room in the mansion. However, we can emotionally suffocate if we pretend sex doesn't have any place at all in our world. It's like the old priest said, "If you have to make a vow of chastity, it's best to make it one day at a time."

Productive Activity:
The Pretty Work of Aware Learning, Doing, Teaching

When you experience created joy in a situation with self, others, or Nature you will discover that productive activity is present, either as aware doing, or as aware learning, or as aware teaching, or as some combination of the three.

Doing is viewed here as the expression of creative relating and sharing. In creative doing there is no aspect of "mistake" possible. Some ways are less effective than are others, but they are not wrong. Stumbles and fumbles are clues for improvement - the aware person simply "does it" differently, more effectively, the next time.

In living a productively active life the purpose of "doing" is not to get finished, but to be socially creative. Life is never done with "doing," so long as you live. With no schedule to get finished pressing against the productively active person, there's no distress in the involvement of living. Creative living is a "do" thing, not a "done" thing.

I learned, to my good fortune, to enjoy work by working with my dad, mother, three sisters, and my brother. I've joked, at times, "My dad, I think, dropped a small hammer into my crib for me to teeth on. Work was my first word." My parents and their generation had a warm and friendly relationship with work. Their lessons, taught through example and the side-by-side joining in doing, were learned early and deeply, and the lessons have endured. Family, as we know, is a primary teacher of character and social values. I find that working with others, Nature, and self is a great way to relate and share. What a marvelous way to spend time... while shaping your character's Q's and A's on the creative-path called living.

The extreme of anything, when that "anything" keeps us from aware inquiry, can become a personality prison. Ignorance and absence of productively active experiences are such extremes. The lack of good teachers early in life can dull a person's edge for inquiry. Fear thrives on dull edges. The absence of good--highly motivated--students makes the best teachers swoon. Mother Nature is about to pass-out, FCOL.

By being present, but unaware, in a situation we miss the lesson being taught, whether we are in the role of student or teacher. With limited awareness, sharing gets lost. Many interpersonal events, affairs, and family arguments have this vacant property: no awareness of the lesson being taught. So also do many personal-self experiences suffer from mal-awareness levels.

Learning is what we humans are designed to do. When learning is occurring, awareness is present and living is a pleasure. Good teachers set the (young) student's confidence and enthusiasm to an eager peak point. When learning is occurring, boredom has no invitation. Class is a composite word of two interchanging, interrelated, interfacing, interacting components: student <u>and</u> teacher; and so, too, is family.

Let me ask you a question, if I may. Which is most dear: education or luxury? Our educational experiences serve us all the moments of our lives; while the luxuries most often fade with time and use. So which is most dear? Which is most ardently pursued?

"There is a great difference," Seneca said, "between not wishing to do evil, and not knowing how." The notion "never tempt the honest" (or you may suffer disappointment) supports the noble idea that to have a healthy society of cooperative individuals we have to be productively active in educating in that direction, and spend less time in blame-placing. Road rage and "bitchin' each other out" are not the hall marks of a healthy society of harmony and balance. But then, who needs quality?

Most people when coming to a narrow crevasse will peer most intently and carefully over the edge, examining the depth; rather than gauging the width. We  stir our fears and doubts about leaping the gap based upon its depth more than upon its width. We seem to be unaware that it is the width that we must master, not the depth. The width is our challenge; the depth is our consequence for misjudgment. In living well we must come to understand that in the "moment-of-truth" of meeting our challenges, it is not our parents, teachers, coaches, therapists, or some writer who must stand the test; we ourselves, alone and absolute, are the masters of our awareness and of our doings, plus or minus. My dad, at my 1955 high school graduation, put it more directly: "A good indication of maturity, son, is when you step in dog shit and you don't look for someone else to blame." I've rarely stepped into crap of any makings, except when unaware. It's not something I usually do for sport. My achievements and my accidents are related to my level of awareness, plus or minus. Stress smothers my awareness and fans my tendency to blame.

Knowing what you are trying to create in a relationship is primary to direction. For example, a classroom teacher is most effective when he/she knows what he/she wants to teach and is aware when situations occur for the application of the lesson. In elementary school we have recess, as we all remember. For what? Exercise? To burn off youthful energy? Yes, certainly. But what about children riding a teeter-totter, or those playing team games? There's more there than physical activity; they're also cooperating and interacting with others. As Gertrude Stein might note: "There is a load of there there." As a teacher you want the children to learn all they can from each experience. Be aware, e.g., of possibilities for social-cooperation practice. In being aware as a teacher, as a student, as a doer your productive activity can light the way for self and others in creating a living path with a heart.

"Know what you are trying to present (to teach) to self and to others," I repeat to myself daily. In every interaction something is taught, something is learned; often several things, depending upon the awareness levels. Some experiences are so pretty we wish we could repeat them, many times; others, we're not so fond of having met. However, awareness enhances every exchange, plus or minus. You will discover peace in living and create joy in doing when productive activity is your daily purpose and companion.

Do not assume that children or adults know how to behave in every situation, however experienced they may be. Letting someone be wrong is easy, not clever. Be smartly creative in showing others how to avoid ineffective or embarrassing behavior. Demonstrate the desired outcome, then permit them to create the means.

When we are weak of character we seem to enjoy seeing others fail and we welcome long-suffering bores who burn themselves at the stake at every opportunity. When weak of character we surround ourselves with "the classes or tribes, too weak to master the flowing conditions of life." (Unknown source) Watch and be aware with whom you spend time; you'll learn something important about self.

In learning situations (especially when reading) do not be a passive passenger, be an active, inquiring student. Don't be a full-time spectator in living, those seats are filled to the overflowing. Laugh, take risks, make mistakes, debate, question, think, engage: participate with awareness. If you don't want others to see you picking your nose, be aware. Look around you before you pick it, if pick it you must, not after you pick it. Plan ahead!

Beware of the advice of peddlers, and charlatans, and self-proclaimed experts! They often deal in fragments and claim their crumbs to be the universe. As Boswell told us, "My brilliant qualities are like embroidery upon gauze...I understand nothing clearly, nothing to the bottom, I pick up fragments, but never have in my memory a mass of any size." Do you know anyone like that? Be aware! The unaware, the naive, the myopic can be fooled by the snake oil of shadows, the dazzle of cheap flash. A point is never broadened by any amount of shake, rattle, and roll... when it veils awareness.

Run your own race. Set your own "best" physical pace and emotional rhythm. How does a person learn this? We hear of "burn-out" from every temple, shrine, and saloon. Is this our "mad-dog" destiny? In the course of daily affairs we view mounds of mute ashes that once were our friends and colleagues: victims of burn-out. And still we do not pace our own efforts. Inanity can take root in the finest of spirits, burn-out can occur in the strongest giants of character. By the time you sense personal burn-out, the coating on your wiring is gone. By the self's first notice, you're already "toast" from rim to hub. Road rage is a hint, spontaneous sobbing is a clue.... Pace is the preventative.

Where do able teachers and models of social pacing assemble? Where does one find them? Today in our fear-ridden, security-based society, few people step forward to savor the valuable risk-experiences of life so vital to balance and harmony of self. Individual responses to risk-events in all the aspects of self keep our edge keen and teach us how to make the strong glue of character found in the spit and sweat of productive activity. We are short-handed when it comes to effective models and teachers in creative living, and the odds against positive social outcome are mounting. To turn this tide of events, a flood-tide of strife, distress, violence, pollution, loneliness, and fear, each of us must seek to become the positive models for future generations. Be productively active in embracing the responsibilities of life's challenges...and share this good fortune with others, and with Nature. When there are no elders, no teachers of pace and wisdom the "villages" of the world become villages of overwhelmed children, and immature choices and purposes become icons.

Positive social role-models give us expanded experiences and good feedback, without which we can end-up practicing <u>mistakes</u> and <u>negative</u> skills in living. Once entangled in bad habits, in order to learn effective social-skills we must first <u>unlearn</u> our negative ones. This is similar to trying to drive a car forward when it is in reverse. Adjustments are needed to proceed... and directional awareness is useful in avoiding major disappointment. But before we argue about where we want to go, may I ask,.. Where are we?

Friends and relatives are not our only teachers. Likewise, our foes can offer us excellent lessons. It is valuable to know and to measure your adversaries well. Our foes can encourage our strongest effort when we respect (accept and recognize) them ; our weakest, when we fear them. This is true for nations as well as for individuals... for quails and eagles, alike.

Some special teachers I've had the good fortune to experience in my life have been: my mom, Irene, my dad, "V", my sisters, Gemma, Joan, and Colleen, my brother, Don, companions Jim Shoemaker and Dave Martin, assorted life-stage friends, teachers, mentors, coaches, loves, school-mates, aspirations and challenges, my children, Carissa, Pam, and Tess and granddaughter Laura, the gang in the clouds, all the baccalaureate personalities (the 2-7's), foes, and pessimistic plodders, and every stranger who ever gave me a smile or a dirty look. We all have a list. Have you reviewed yours recently? Are you making daily additions? Oh, let me include Nod Skrap and Ivan Franzen.

Do a task to be doing it, not to get it done. Do each task as if it is being done for yourself,.. for, indeed, it is. Have you ever had the pleasure of having a mechanic work on your car as if it were his car? A rare event but pure joy when it occurs, don't you agree? Do each task with patient awareness. But as a Chinese fellow (I wish I could remember his name) once said, "Do not seek perfection or you'll never complete the book (task)." If I write: Hope is the doer's companion... and many are his/her willing dance-partners," have I planted the seeds of an adage, or those of a myth?

Clarence Darrow (him, I remember) is supposed to have said, "Anyone who is an optimist after thirty is a fool, and anyone who is a pessimist before thirty is too damned smart." If Mr. Darrow was an older (over thirty) non-optimist as his words indicate, why did he bother to say anything that might be taken as instructive? A teacher of the first stripe has to be optimistic about the human potential to learn, to change, and to influence positively the course of human existence. Was Mr. Darrow speaking in bitter hindsight or hopeless foresight? Was he seeking mass suicide or mass applause? Such comments numb me. I'd rather be coaxed toward awareness. How about you? What's your rather?

I've found foresight to lean toward hopeful when, through the aware experience of productive activity, a person honors wisdom and respects change. Hindsight then becomes the memory of positive pleasure, not a scar of regret or criticism. I, for one, don't need anyone prodding me to become snide, pessimistic, hollowed-out, or pissed-off in my social perception. I can manage this on my own. I've had all the practice I want in the trait of "social trashing." Life is often like Winston Churchill's manor wall, of which he said, "Any damn fool can see what's wrong with it. What is right with it?" What's right with your life? Are you building a personal pyramid with the stones of your Present challenges, or are you using them to bitterly lapidate, from ambush, the Future dreams of self and others?

Some people depend on the talents and social values developed through productive activity; some depend on the "kindness of strangers" (ala Tennessee William's Blanche); others depend on luck. "They can hum the melody, but they don't know the words" is a fitting description of most "bees" in our global-hive. Living is experience dependent. Living well is <u>big-time</u> aware-experiential. When left with instructions to perform, but with no direct guidance regarding how, we flounder. Don't expect others or self to be able to do what you/they have no experience doing. A great choir with no direction can be an ungreat mob. Experience and evolution both start with the same letter, so, too, do creation and crisis.

A minute of "doing" is worth 24 hours of TV-ing. Our young children and teens talk on the telephone for hours, often telling lies about things they could be doing if they weren't talking on the telephone telling lies. Do life, don't merely talk about it, don't simply watch it. Be productively active. Build your verb-enriched pyramid, dance with others who are likewise invested, and keep your eyes on the eagle.

Television gives us instant company, but mostly it teaches us little. At the flick of a switch our lonely world is less empty, but no dialogue or exchange of ideas is possible. This must be why many people like and use call-in shows on both radio and television. Loneliness, our personal phantom, is chased by the noise of taped voices and cathode-ray images. At TV's party we learn little, we do less, and we teach nothing but "couch surfing." Where's the productive activity? Where's the awareness? When television (any visual media) and productive activity come to blend, and this has happened on occasion,.. ah, the social potential fills the "winds of change" with a fragrance of loam.

To "veg" occurs without any skill or effort on our parts, and this absence of involvement sets up a cycle of a recurring problem of loneliness. When we're seriously close-dancing with awareless television, we're not only not aware of "real" others, we're not even in touch with "self." When you shut-off the television your physical-self usually goes to "pee." What does your loneliness do? It asks you to dance, what else? Loneliness will dance with any taker.... Talk about zero shame.

Humor is the key to positive change in one's path toward productive activity. When the burdens of living have you taking detours into dead-ends away from productive activity resuscitate your Sense of Humor. When you seek learning and discovery in your relationships stir in humor. Respect, enjoy, and dance with others, self, and Nature: what a nice recipe for living. Productive activity is, on the dance floors of good living, the "Big Show." Oh, did you notice--resuscitate is a verb, FCOL?

Respect (acceptance and recognition) of self, others, and Nature is reflected in our awareness and good manners...especially when alone at home. When we're alone is when many of our attitudes and habits are sculpted. Respect and courtesy are to relationship as oil is to an engine. Living works much better with courtesy toward and respect for Nature, self and others. Either socially or when alone bad thoughts, bad attitudes, and bad breath have a lot in common. By the way, how exactly does a person show respect and good manners toward our dear mother, Nature? Any ideas? I think she's waiting.

Many people have said, "The more I learn, the less I know." But large, too, is the crowd of us who know little without a whit of learning effort: "They know nothing simply as a generous gift of Nature," said our old friend Benedetto Croce.

To reach the pinnacle of maturity a person must climb the steep, muddy hill called aware-living. The slope steepens at about age ten years and the footing becomes less stable. Some people endure the slippin' and slidin', proceeding upward and onward creating a model for others; others stop, sink unhappily into the mud and become obstacles and snags for those coming-up behind them. They view Tennyson's "...silent pinnacles of aged snow" from distant despair, and they turn, unthrilled, from the challenges of contending, contributing, and cooperating.

Since we are all somewhat different from each other there will always be some friction in living and there is risk involved when you take a stand against the prevailing social currents. Respect, patience and humor are the social lubricants most useful for productively active social-cooperation. If you spit into the wind, expect to get some back on you. So why spit? Why wear attitude-gray?

A theme song that I like for productively active people is: "We're off to see the Wizard, the wonderful Wizard of **Do**." Could you hum a few bars while we dance?

Or perhaps you know the words.

Situational - Contextual Awareness
Common Sense Strikes Again
and Again... and Again

As jugglers-in-living each of us have three balls in motion at all times: the ball that <u>was</u> (the past), the ball that <u>is</u> (the present), and the ball that <u>will be</u> (the future). With age the ball that <u>was</u> and the ball that <u>will be</u> expand and shrink in size respectively (our past gets larger; our future, smaller). Our expectations are rooted in our memories of the past. Our hopes are fingers of sunlight that extend into the darkness of the future. Productive activity, which can occur only in the present, is the balance wheel of our expectations and our hopes. The future actually has no guaranteed time-size. Dreams and hopes are but tiny flares shot into the immense darkness. This awareness is the thing that religions, and myths, and human courage are made of.

To look fixedly into the past to the denial of the present and the future is one of life's worst scams. No one said to us, "Here is a life-span of time - go waste it!" Without an investment in the present, there is no future. Suicide, the killing of self, takes many forms... some are more sudden than others. Suicide is a personal declaration that the future is perceived as a valueless void. Suicide is a vote cast against the future.

Do not allow the past to hold your present and your future in chains. Living is an on-going, on-doing process that is continuous. Living is not completed at some set age or by some particular event, such as marriage, retirement, death of a loved one, etc. Living stops at your death. Awareness stops at your death. Relationship--the creating of opportunity <u>and</u> value--stops at your death. The future (time) stops at your death. We are told: "In life nothing ever stays the same. In death nothing ever changes." The time indexes of Past, Present, and Future seem to be a Life-thing, not a Death-thing,.. so use them while you can.

It is not possible to work-on yesterday, today, and tomorrow all at the same time. "Today," it has been said, "is that time passing between yesterday and tomorrow." It is more even than that. The present is the fulcrum of your living continuum. The Past, the Present, and the Future (PPF) may appear to be separable, but only on clocks, if then.... In the swirling context of self-creating there is no actual separation. Remove one... if you can. And if you could, what do you have left? I'm interested in your thoughts on this wee item... so, please, flame-up your lantern and wave it at me. Let's meet for coffee and a chat.

Nalli

There is a huge difference between having a "sense of history" and in having "your head stuffed-up your past." The future is a human construct that is planned and designed in the present; just as the present was shaped in the past. Preparation, within limits short of obsessive-compulsive nut-harvesting, ia a major ingredient in Opportunity's Pie. To have dreams and goals of what you are willing to strive for is one common definition of future... to have your "head in the clouds" holds yet another meaning. In cliff-climbing it is warned: "Don't look down (back)!" The rest of the climb is ahead of you, not behind you. It's the same in living. Don't cheat yourself out of tomorrow by dwelling permanently in yesterday. Use your yesterdays to indicate your past abilities and purposes. Let your future be where you hang your immediate and long-term goals, and let your present be where you evaluate and match your past and current abilities with your future ambitions. The common sense approach is-- have balance and harmony in your PPF mix for personality-wellness.

Living is strained and strange when you always look at today's reality and tomorrow's dreams with yesterday's eyes. Today is where the action is, yesterday is where the experience is, and the future... ah, the future... it can seem a dragon in ambush for those without the present-moment's personal-creation of opportunity and value. Without healthy relationship the relentless press of the future can frazzle your resolve like coarse sandpaper on parchment. Without healthy relationship the weight of the past can smother your awareness like damp sand packed down your throat. Individualism, isolation, and absolute independence do not form a long parade of friends. Parades of collective-community that express common values and opportunity, that have a march-step of balance and harmony across the full-range of Past, Present, and Future, require healthy relationship, self-awareness, and productive activity.

Models

Preparation and practice are not only useful in living an effective life, they are necessary for it. Pick your companions and models well, and don't wait for a crisis before you begin to act, to prepare, and to practice. Don't wait until you're lost in a deep swamp of misery to begin paying attention to your surroundings and to your passage. It is a foolish ship's captain who waits to have his first lifeboat drill <u>after</u> the ship is sinking. Chaos has a rude way of interrupting daily performance. Your choice's offsprings can become highly riotous if you ignore, neglect, or otherwise abuse them.

The people with whom we spend our time and energy (in the flesh, print, video, etc.) have a major influence on how we might choose to live. To have good posture it helps to have models of good posture; to have good ideas, good-idea models; to have a good attitude, a good-attitude model. Even good models need models. Humans are a chain of learning...one generation to the next. This is not an issue of blame, this is an issue of positive outcome. What will we teach today? What will we learn? What will we practice? Motivated good players give good continuous outcome; bad mates, bad results. As Casey Stengel asked, "Isn't there anyone on this team who knows how to play the game?"

Watch for people, of all ilk and age, who might teach you steps to try on the path to self knowledge. Don't be overly impressed by the words of "experts" regarding life management skills; see if living is working for them. Be aware! Dance with many... once, but ask few to join you for a stroll. You don't get to choose your parents and family, but you do get to vote on models.

In life's dramatic-comedy each person is both an actor and a spectator. As one spectates, one likewise acts; as one acts, one likewise spectates. If not, then we're talking about a broccoli plant, not an aware person. How do you and broccoli get along?

In living do not be concerned with being famous. Be involved with being <u>interesting</u> and <u>interested</u>. The act of good living does not need anyone to be famous, but it does need interesting and interested participants. Life is famously dull without these qualities.

Have you noticed how quickly children learn to <u>complain</u> and <u>blame</u>? There must be a lot of models showing them the way, huh? How many times have you complained or blamed today? This week? Is carping in the genes, or is it another learned social-addiction? Could we be talking "crutches" here?

If the only tool a child (a person) has is a hammer, then he/she will see all issues in living as a nail. He/she will beat on life rather than learning to be a creative artist or craftsperson. Increase your tools, increase your skills through experience and awareness... preparation and practice.

It is difficult to give up the belief that technology is the "magic hammer" and the sole solution to the problems in living. A computer in every crib? That'll do it! But where do we get the character-development software? Our technological intoxication/addiction has us believing that the tools, skills, and information for "making a living" are the same tools, skills, and information neccessary and sufficient for creating opportunity and values. This is a major **NOT**!

We have become devout believers that an educated person is one who spends his/her time studying and memorizing what others (a few) have said about living, about the world, about the universe, about the deities of heaven and hell. Such information can be useful, as history tends to be, but it is not sufficient. The educated person heeds the lessons from the past and seeks to blend them with his/her knowledge of current social and natural information and experiences. The educated person steadily builds his/her pyramid and eagerly strolls a creative path. For the educated person the challenge of knowing self is danced with gladly, using respect, patience, productive activity, and humor to chase fear. There are no childish, fear-streaked mysteries for the creative, mature Doer. There are just exciting possibilities. The aware Doer knows that many people don't have a "chicken-fried clue" when it comes to "soaring with the eagles."

Just because an attitude was held in high regard by a former generation does not give it, necessarily, a permanent place of honor in current use or acceptance. Social attitudes need more to recommend them than a history of existence. Do not fear change. To fear change is to fear living. But know it fully--change has a cost, a risk, and often meets with stiff resistance from others. To adjust your social attitude while engaged in the spinning-current of living is not so unlike changing saddles on a horse upon which you are riding that is running at a full gallop. The only game you can play without doing anything is the "Game of Duh." No one on this side of the print is telling you that being a model is all warm and fuzzy... or in building your pyramid you won't "pop" a few blisters. Look for your models on <u>both</u> sides of your personality.

<u>Blame</u>

Nothing deserves less time than blame; scratch it from your "do" list. To blame is to live in the past. In the pursuit of creating a path with a heart, blame is the great detour.

The saying goes: "If the shoe fits, wear it!" But remember, if the foot stinks, then before long so will the shoe. You become what you associate with (and "waxie worsa" as my young daughter used to say), so let those "fitting" shoes beware. Blame won't chase the stink... blame <u>is</u> stink.

Blame is the "black-hole" of relationship. It cuts opportunity's throat and it rapes sharing. Blame is the 1st cousin of Denial, a couple of primitive little "rednecks," not real-cool dance-partners. They're both as silly and immature as licking "bug-splats" from a hot windshield. When the creative elements are missing in the events of living, you'll hear heavy "bitching." A cacophony of "care and woe" bitching will rattle your bones and ravel the seams of your soul, when enthusiasm and cooperation have to "duke it out" with relentless distress in a joyless fight. To be blame-less start out by being blame-free. Give blame the "shortest-of-shrifts," give blame the boot.

In our posthaste, "yupped-up" world, we now have found a host upon which to blame all our ills--Stress. Stress is often silent and usually invisible. Blame has a perfect goose... or is that, ghost? What a "beaut" Stress is... and isn't. Stress is neither clever, nor selective. It can spread and cover in one coat. No brush marks, no DNA traces.

When you feel a finger being stuck up your nose, more often than not it's your own. That's been my experience with fingers and noses. Know what I mean? Blame who? Blame when? Blame what? Why blame? Already I've spent far too much time on this blame business... but where can I hang the responsibility? Who can I blame? I'll accept volunteers.... Ah, thank goodness, here comes Stress.

Goals

Goal setting doesn't give a person the motivation to create a pathway of achieving the goal. A goal provides a direction, not the motivation. We err in seeking motivation from our goals. We falsely set goals hoping to become motivated. It does not work well that way; too often, we fall flat. Consider the mountains of unmet New Year's resolutions (goals) that have been uttered down through human history. Why unmet? Lack of motivation. The goals were clear enough, but it was all words, no "do." All direction, no creative energy. All talking, no walking.

To set a goal at which to direct your behavior does not provide you the means, or the motive, for obtaining that goal. To set a goal is to make a decision; but to set a goal, is not to achieve it. The shortest distance between the two points of (1) goal setting and (2) achievement is aware application of living experience and knowledge. If you have no such experience or knowledge, then it can indeed be a "Long way to Tipperary."

A goal is what you set as a suggested stopping-point from which to set your next goal, should you decide upon one. Focus upon the motivation; that urge-desire to squeeze the trigger, moment-to-moment, in your attempt to hit the target (the goal). As there is a huge divide between Reach and Grasp, there is a far yawn between Goals and Motivation.

What are your choices, your values, your motivation? Do not set goals when you are not aware of your context. To set goals without context awareness is as ineffective as gargling air to cure strepp throat. Seek to mate your choices and goals to your values and motivation. To set goals without intent and action is an empty exercise. And while a clue to self, it is not a "hard resource" to creative living. Good goal setting and achievement result from solid self-knowledge and context-awareness. Tally-ho, the fox is running!

Mood Management

Be aware of self, others and Nature.

I once saw a poster picturing a train track, or it may have been a country road, which said, "Life is a journey, not a destination." Living is an experiment, not a result. Living is a changing flow of events, some call them problems that seek solutions. Whatever the mood, living is not a mosaic of pre-set certainty. Loneliness, and its house-pet "Boredom," can be found rooted in the arid desert called: fear of change. Of course, some people seem to prefer a life-time of "poop-scooping" Boredom's droppings over chasing Fear... even once.

"To him who is in fear, everything rustles," observed Sophocles. (Gosh, I like those Greek names.) You certainly don't have to repeat old Sophocles' words to anyone who, as a youngster, has spent a night alone in a creaky house in the country. Picture the scene: A moonless, wind-swept, creepy, damp-lonely night. The mood for a quivering youth: Fear-rustling Halloween-heavy every... single... bug-eyed second. Regretably, "Boo Time" lasts an insecure life-time for far too many people. When fear asks them to dance they shiver as if clad "in the garb of a barefooted Carmelite (Long-fellow)," and they choose to be of helpless mien as they, gaped-mouth and rigid, watch a Humpty-Dumpty world teeter and topple SMACK! onto their "Chicken-Little" moods. Blame comes easily to the lips of Fear's serfs.

Making changes and taking risks are scary ventures. Like not wanting to leave the security of a night-time campfire in a jungle; where, out in the darkness, you hear the sounds and silence, real and imagined, of danger... it's eminently understandable. Dark is dark, but some dark is darker than is other dark. But nothing is <u>so</u> dark that a friend can't help brighten it... if you'll choose to permit it. Your "mood of the moment" is listed on your "Choice Menu" .... Look it over.

"Happy are those who dream, and are ready to pay the price to make them come true." (Cardinal Suenens of Belgium) I like it. To "pay the price," however, means productive activity, not cash or credit. Risk taking, like parachuting, always has a period of free-fall before the chute opens... it comes <u>after</u> you jump. There are no absolute guarantees. If there were, it's not a risk.

A person climbs the mountains in living in order to find new valleys. You can't enjoy the valleys, if you're not willing to climb the mountains. The "Sweat Equity Rule" holds: Those who stay in a low valley see only the looming impossibility of the mountains, while those who choose to create an upward-moving path have the option to see the fruitful possibilities of endless valleys and meadows... and they gain strength of self and character from the rigors of the mountains.

Just as the "soup can be only as tasty as the ingredients you put into it," so, too, living is a reflection of what you put into it. For that nice touch of fun, be sure to sprinkle in the humor. Humor keeps the blisters from hurting quite so much.

Laughter comes easier when you know what you're seeking and when friends join you in the chase. Everyone enjoys sliding down a laugh, now and then. So seek to "give yourself a more balanced personality this year and every year to come." Personal goals that include respect for others and Nature offer rhythm-setting keys to mood's choice-points. Your mood directly reflects your awareness, patience, and respect regarding your flowing context and its contents. "Road Rage," for example, does not reflect harmony, way too jagged, lumpy, and reactive. Screaming in the street is <u>not</u> community singing.

Once we have made a decision to create a path of particular direction and duration, we cannot take another dissimilar path at the same time. Choice points and context are well worth our awareness energy. But today many people seem to expect the music to create all the mood, and luck to put all the spin on the ball. Another "Blame Format" is born. Fact is, mood <u>is</u> the music <u>and</u> the spin; mood works both ends, the middle, and all the complex sides, parameters, and dimensions of context... and context works mood. Thales certainly knew how to pick tough mountains. Mount Self is a "grinnin' monster" of challenges.

Personality is a social term: a definition relative to one's <u>inter</u>personal cooperation skills and efforts. Relating and sharing are the artful essences of being/doing human. Creating self and discovering context are life-long adventures of awareness. Living starts early, ends late in your life-span. The streets named Self and Context are both life-long creative hikes...best done with others and Nature.

"One of the deep secrets of life is that all that is really worth doing is what we do <u>for</u> others." (Lewis Carroll) It appears that Mr. Carroll, who is famous for his imaginative tales of a day-dreaming Alice, rabbit holes, and looking glasses, also held some nice ideas about the adventures in relating. You may have noticed Mr. Carroll didn't put an age-limit on this behavior.

To invite Despair to mate with your mood, to hang your "sword and shield on the wall," to say, "Let's put out the fires and call in the hounds. The hunt is over!" are errors in the direction of Depression. As long as you live, there is living to do, self to create, context to discover.

No bridge is to be found erected spanning the abyss between our hopes and our fulfillment. Each of us must build his/her own passage plank by plank, cable by cable, stone by stone with each other person we encounter and with Nature. Sometimes we do well, sometimes we stumble and fumble. Such events define life's struggle. So remember: "Adversity is not defeat."

"All evil is disharmony: between man and Nature, or man and men, or man and himself." (Mr. Will Durant again) When a person has patient maturity and friendly dignity in his/her daily social affairs, that is when life's song sounds potential and hope.

When you discover that you share no common social values with a person, e.g., you disagree strongly with the personal motives and social goals expressed, what are your choices? Do you have to sit down to dinner with "a Hitler," when you cannot suffer what the person represents? Create value in such cases by accepting and recognizing self and acting with mature responsibility. To respect self it is important to know self, to manage a mood which makes your eyes glow with enthusiasm for learning, teaching, doing it is important to embrace a goal of productive activity. How do you do that??? Ah!.. that is your mission. How's your mood?

To change your behavior it is helpful if you behave in a changed way. You can't just talk about changing, you must do change. How's that for a simple obvious? Of course, you must do your "do" in aware ways for best results.

As you know you can't draw a line in the sand (of your beliefs) without disturbing the sand. Change is the natural flow and outcome of living. Every wave, sooner or later, hits the beach. Nothing lasts forever, no matter how sweet it seems or perfect in its moment. It is because of this "rule of change" that dependency is not a free ride. Dependency keeps a person in fear of change: afraid of the natural flow of living. Do not ride on the efforts and preparations of others, for when the crash, the flop, the flip, the slide come, and they will come you'll have no context awareness, no understanding of self, no mood managing skills. You'll be butt-naked in a storm of change... and you'll likely cling to the next passing post. Living is not surfing; you have to do more in living - to live well- than to wait for a new wave to catch. In living in a free society, it takes socially aware and responsible decisions by each person if we are to create the good rather than the bad. To pick a direction, to create opportunity and values, to have self and context awareness, to set your own rhythm and mood... Hey!.. you've got to practice.

Do you, or anyone you know, have a fear of making decisions? A fellow named Walter Kaufman has called this fear: "Decidophobia." Sounds like a disease a tree might have, huh? Does having a label for a specific fear give us a special magic in erasing that fear? Labels only give us words to use in talking about our fears. Nice, but words change nothing. Changes in living, choice-points awareness and active decisions occur only in response to doing. Our "media I.V." addiction has us kneeling before an altar of actionless words and "hip-shot" opinions. Our social mood is in a free-fall plunge... and we flick-on the "tube," hoping "words" will fill the void and chase away the fright. It will never happen. "Main line" actions, not words.

Many of us are brought-up in the belief that to show "love" for others we must "worry" for them. This hatches mutual dependency and entrapment, not love and sharing. Neither person experiences joy or freedom in such an exchange. A fresher path is: "To share with, but not to worry for; to respect, but not to control; to trust self, so that you can trust others."

You can never <u>guarantee</u> another person's emotional well-being. Do not, in some disarming moment of passion or crippling parental concern, get lured into that dungeon of human mis-involvement of mythical emotional-miracle-working. It cannot be done. The neurotic knots cannot be loosened from the outside by others or by Nature. We're each in charge of our own moods, motives, actions, and fears. For you to guarantee "happiness" in a character-rooted neurotic is as silly as trying to strain spinach through a cat. Who invented all this imaginary "personal" power anyway? Who believes it?

We own no one; we aren't even renting them. Relating is most precious when interlaced with sharing: creating opportunity while creating value. Without the sweet song of sharing, mutual space-occupation often results in sharp elbowing and vented anger. Of such flash points war rumbles, divorce resonates, and road rage roils. "Rumble, resonate, and roil" are the "shake, rattle, and roll" of anger.

Anger always believes it is right. Anger, as usually expressed, is a self-interested act which fails to check with others and tramples the fences of social propriety and good manners. Anger, when shrieking at its own agony, has a blind sense of absoluteness. Anger, when whispering at its own contempt, is a serious gossip. Anger's roots are fear; it is the voice of fear. Do not use your anger to drive others away from you; use your anger to know self. Anger tracks directly to your fear; fear tracks to self. Be aware of the "hot-line" opportunity to self when your mood moves to "mad." Tap-in, trace, and take-notes. Oh, by the way, it isn't smart for little "us" to get too "pissed or peaked" at BIG Mother Nature. She sets her own rhythm, doesn't really care about our pouts, and may crush us with a shrug.

Set your own emotional rhythm. Don't get caught-up in the negative currents of other people's anxiety and neurotic episodes. Tell the neurotics in your living events: "Take your tantrums somewhere else, plea-se!" Mother Nature taught me this in First Grade. I was a little slow. I didn't learn everthing that I needed to know in Kindergarten. How'd you do? I'm <u>still</u> learning, FCOL.

No one can live your life for you, better than you can live it for yourself. However, many will try. You are the only one who is there for <u>all</u> the choice points. The light ones, the bright ones, the dark ones, and the pitch-black ones. Beware of blindly acting on doxy, and thinking you're making aware choices. Doxy, at times, can be pure ebony.

A person shows strength of character when he/she holds others up for praise, not when he/she holds others down through scorn and prejudice. Creating opportunity and value are the purest acts of respect for self, others, and Nature. Set your rhythm based upon aware personal, social, and ecological choices and your mood's harvest will reap abundantly and your spirit's hearth-fire will glow warmly.

Be involved in living! Be active on the field of play! Most of us "sits" deep in the life's spectators' stands waiting for a random "foul ball" to land in our picnic basket. Then we have a false thrill of participation. To "sits" is not to dance. Know self and offer your time and energy, your life, in productive activity to others and Nature... that is to dance.

Each day is a fresh "opportunity-creating" chance to the optimist, but just another dip in the cesspool to the pessimist. Pessimists are not known to speak eagerly of creating anything.... But they know the dark side of the moon rather well. If you want to know about darkness couple-up with pessimism. Mood-mugging is assured. I've visited there.

Be aware of the language you use, the language you think in, and the language you keep in storage for listening and as a reference library. Is the language you spin optimistic or pessimistic? Is it divisive and deceptive or relational and explanatory? Is your language pool a one-dimensional tool in a confused game of reactive living, or is it a window into a four-five-or-six dimensional game of productive activity? Check your Q & A inventory and keep it fresh and refreshing.

Be inside of what you do. If you work, be inside, not outside, of the work; if you play music, be inside of the music; if you are a student, be inside of your studies. Be inside of living; create it, make it yours. Be aware of situations and contexts! Be aware of mood and manner, of purpose and priority, of the Grinch and of the Three Men in the Tub. As "Fatigue can make cowards of us all (Vince Lombardi)," so Fear depresses and ladles on the laziness.

One major thing wrong with loafing, or plodding through life, is that there isn't much challenge in it, and you learn little, teach little, and do little. You're productively sterile for all the time and energy spent. The last time I checked, time is a limited quantity in life... and so is energy. Mood manage them with humor, respect, and patience. You'll create a living path that's one friend shy of a perfect romance.

If everything were ideal without effort on our part, we would have no creative role and living would be intolerable yawn. A Scottish saying about preparation and effort is worth heeding: "No time is wasted sharpening your sickle." This is about living effectively. Keep your tools (knowledge, understanding, awareness) keen; it makes your daily toil a more cooperative event. Trashing "Paradise" may have been God's greatest gift to us. Of course, I might be wrong. So far we haven't danced well with the challenge.

Just as surely as nothing can be built enduringly upon fear and hate; so too, can nothing ever be lost that is rooted in love, and nurtured in sharing. Balance in living comes through the productive activity of creating opportunity (relating) and creating value (sharing) with self, others and Nature using situational/contextual awareness. In relating and sharing, as in sports performance, the more you practice the more often the "magic" happens. Mood is manageable, life is livable, and a path with a heart is possible. Heck, if we keep working on our pyramids, God and Mother Nature may just put us (back) on their Guest Lists.

Save not one drop of life's oil in order to light your path in death. What we call our "path" is the living of life. To ask: "Does our path have a heart?" is to seek our collective social aspect of self. Our social aspect is our heart in living.

Relating and sharing with self, others, and Nature are the remedies for fear, loneliness and pollution. Hold social and ecological purpose as a priority, know self in all its aspects, be a friend, and let the wind and the rain of challenge blow and be welcome in your hair--you'll be of merry mood and meter. Situational/contextual awareness is a primary guide for effective people in developing a personal formula for living that includes maturity, love, fun, and heart. **Be Aware! Seek Balance, Harmony, and Peace.**

Humor a la mode

In cooking spaghetti it's a popular practice, when readiness-testing, to toss some against a wall. In writing a book, the wall is your personality; the spaghetti, words.... And at times, in this book, words with small amounts of eagle guano mixed-in. In writing, both the wall and the pasta are being tested to see if anything sticks, to whom, or to what.

All normal humans have the physical ability to "make a laugh." Sense of Humor is not at the surface of a laugh, it is at the base. Merely to physically "make a laugh," especially at others pain, at smut, or at chaos, or at misfortune is not the light of a bright Sense of Humor. Hyenas laugh, but they are not known for having a Sense of Humor... or for coming-up with clever, subtle punchlines. Hyenas just "make a laugh." Humor and laughter are not necessarily the same thing. Too often laughter/expresses a State of Nerves, not a Sense of Humor.

A Chinese proverb tells us, "Pity those who laugh too much, for they are always unhappy." Let's not rush to equate absolutely laughter with Sense of Humor. My extended-family's representative "Grump" used to scoff, "There's lotsa' laughter in the saloons of the world without much sign of humor." "Sense of Humor," it is argued by some, "is, indeed, a Sense." As taste, smell, touch, etc., are senses. Why do we call it a Sense, if it is not a Sense? Perhaps, we should say: "Not-a-sense of Humor."

On the hike along my personal path in living, I've noticed that we humans laugh loudest, longest, and hardest at what scares us deep, deeper, and deepest. Is this Humor at play with our Care and Woe? In today's effort to explain and to paint-over with words, and more words, those things that we don't understand... we tend to blend humor and wit. Have you visited those words in a "diction-ary bar," lately? An interesting blend this stir of word-pigments. And now we have a new term, in old dress, that we don't understand. Sense of Humor is but one of many word-groups that we toss freely at "walls," near and far, to express and test life's events with scant idea what our tongues flip, our pens drip, or our key-boards clop. Some other words of high use, low understanding are: Gravity, time, God, electricity, love, appetite, addiction, intelligence,... Enough!

At this point, let us apply our minds' chisels to roughing-out a definition of Sense of Humor as might fit into the frame-work and coffin-box of this book. I'll go first... by saying that Humor is an appetite. (But two unknowns do not make a known, duh-man Mike.) Humor is a need just as food, drink, sleep, sex, exercise, problem-solving, usw., are needs. A person can get Humor-horny just as she/he can get chocolate-horny,.. or popcorn-horny,.. or nap-horny,.. or hug-horny.

Now, to mold this book's concepts into a clay-like model of Sense of Humor, I offer to you the effect and the affect, the yes and the no, the giddy-up and the whoa, the Q and the A of the Four Hoes-men of Relationship: Physical well-being, emotional well-being, mental well-being, and (awareness) contextual well-being. These Four Hoes by creating a concert of harmony and balance through social cooperation, respect, patience, and productive activity with others and Nature give face and form to our Spiritual Self. This expressive harmony and balance of Spirit is also called Sense of Humor. Spirit, I believe, is motive to create a living path. A doctor once said, "Laugh 100 times a day for good health." Holy ulcers!.. was he serious? Exercise your Sense of Humor, to be sure... but to laugh 100 times a day, FCOL. How about 87 times, or 103? How am I doing, Doc? Humor-pressure okay, is it? Is my Spirit high or low?

No one else, but you, can teach, school, or personally train your Sense of Humor. You be da guru. You cultivate the expression of your Sense of Humor through the contextual experiences and understanding of living that you create in your daily productive activity. One's productive activity determines a person's path of choice in living. Productive activity is, to the creative, challenge-embracing individual, far more smiles than sweat. Humor is the active dance of respect for others and for Nature. Our Sense of Humor is our patient awareness of life's challenges... and an optimistic lean toward Hope.

By its nature Hope is optimistic,.. and Humor is Hope, in aware action. Humor is a direct, clear window into Self and all of its aspects. The brighter a person's Sense of Humor the more you can know about the living choices available in a context-flow for creating a relationship with that person. "To feel Humor's grace," some say, "be at peace and in harmony with Nature," Whenever I greet Nature, whatever her mood, with a smile of relaxed confidence I do feel... well, yes... grace-filled and courageous. I think Ernest Hemingway would like that last little add-on about courage. And when I talk of Choice's Philosophy with others, especially when they are in a sharp Q & A mood, I feel cheerful and energized. A good discussion with friends-of-the-Spirit is more pumping than 50 cups of pure-bean caffeine. Leave an extra chair or space for Humor and it will surely join you. Humor is the voice of your spirit.... And Spirit creates Humor's flow. I've never heard God or Mother Nature laugh, but "insiders" claim that they both, being huge of Spirit, possess notable Senses of Humor. This reminds me of a dentist I go to. He doesn't laugh much... ever... but he has a neat spirit about him. He's the sort of person who can make a root canal fun. Really. Humor is responsibility to be shared.

Humor is a main guardrail on the path of good living. Awareness is the center guideline. Patience and Respect are the margins' warning-stripes, and Productive Activity is the bridge to Hope's high-ground. With these character traits in place we can stroll our living pathway,.. staying out of the ditches, the briars, and the swamp ponds of blame, gossip, no hope, and denial. Concentration, the art-form of being aware, alert, and relaxed all at the same time, is a boon, a special human gift-ability, to effective, orderly living.... And Humor is a top-notch expression of concentration.

Egad, I'm still defining. Let's fly back over the wake-site and see how the Content of the definition fits the form of the coffin-box. Expressing Sense of Humor is not just, simply, only,.. merely laughing,.. as some would like to believe. Much laughter is sparked by silly things, socially unhealthy things. Humor's edge of bright awareness is found in one's eagerness of Spirit in engaging the challenges in creating her/his daily living-path. <u>All</u> the <u>fun</u> in living comes from greeting the challenge of the moment and asking it to dance. To laugh, or not to laugh those are our options... a personal crossroad. Simply because someone laughs at an event does not assure that a bright-eyed Sense of Humor dwells within; nor does no laughter, necessarily, equate to no Sense of Humor. Don't write-off Grumpy Dwarf until you try spending some productively active time with him. He may add in all dimensions to your pyramid.

The secret to dealing with difficult times and with dancing close to seemingly impossible issues is: Toss them over the fence into Humor's yard. Humor can melt down any fear. That's what the Human Spirit is all about. Now that's <u>funny</u>.... That is definitely fun.

Hans Selye, the father of the Stress-in-Living concept, defined a humor-less situation as: Stress. Originally an engineering term for external pressure in a set situation, Selye used the term to include internal pressure... a "sciencish-term" for distress... in a science-adored time. Science, to my knowledge, has never been accused of being particularly witty, humorous, or funny. I have never noticed

Numbers having a Sense of Humor. Selye would agree, I suggest, that, since you and I are an active, additive part of the context in which we live, how we perceive the flow, internal and external, determines whether, to us, an event is fear-filled, neutral, humorous, humor-less, stress-rich,.. or a yawn.

W. C. Fields, the actor of renowned, sardonic drunkenness, said, "Start each day with a smile--and get it over with." Could he have been addressing bureaucrats, bikers, joggers, and people waiting in supermarket check-out lines? Whatever your Sense of Humor's exercise-choice keep it limber, relaxed, and toned. A fit Sense of Humor is a marvelous companion in a shoot-out with Stress. And while anxiety has no permanent camp in the land of the humorous, Stress can "call you out" at any time without drum-roll or warning.

"Modesty and humor--seeing the part in light of the whole--are good vaccines against (metaphysical) madness." (From Will Durant in his Interpretations of Life, p. 153.) Likewise, we are told, "Cheerfulness promotes health and immortality. Cheerful people live longest here on Earth, afterward in our hearts." (Mr. or Mrs. anonymous,.. book and page unknown.) To be cheer-filled and anxiety-filled in the same life-time/moment is to offer the world a pucker, rather than a grin. Personally, I prefer dancing with the cheery ones over the chary ones, the bright ones over the dull ones.

Well, I've tossed a load of words at your wall. Did anything stick that was to your liking or disappointment? I'll close the tossing by quoting Patti Wooten, who said, "Humor may or may not add years to your life, but it does add life to your years." "Hmmm," sayeth my cup.

Listed below are exercises in Humor-stretching. Try one-a-day for 13 days,.. then recycle or add your own. Feel free to toss your guano-pasta at my wall, if you will. I'm interested. My personality is eager to see what sticks. Hey, I'm hungry. Would you pass the Humor, please?

Titles to think about. Hitch a ride! Create your own active, fun short-stories or poems about living:

"The Hounds are on my Heels" about daily stresses and how to shake them through humor and love.

"The Sixty-Second Minute" about taking living in your hands and enjoying it; accepting both the bad seconds and the good seconds.

"Detours From my Dreams" about the energy we put into running from our dreams because of fear.

"A Knowing Laugh" about wisdom hatched from aware experiences.

"Get Your Oars in the H_2O" about active productivity. We're not special angels sent by God to watch "living" happen.

"Let's Stamp-Out Loneliness" about our number one social problem and creating relationship as a remedy-skill.

"Acquaintances in a Conspiracy" about two people seeking to create relationship.

"They Don't Run in Herds, You Know" about special, creatively social people being rare; befriend them when you can.

"Hell Can Be a Very Small Place" about hell being the backrooms in the lonely person's mind. The rooms are despair, apathy and depression.

"Some People Are a Real Pain in the Laugh" about relationship being a humorous mystery of choice points.

"The Campfire of Friendship" about the circle of warmth and light provided by friends.

"In the Game of Life, Death is Always the Ace of Trump" about...(whatever you decide).

"If Human Souls Did Never Kiss and Greet" (John Keats) about relationship being the golden thread of living.

A title can often be like a brief, memorable poem. I enjoy discovering and creating interesting titles. If you have titles that are special, please, let me hear from you.

A closing wave: These final words are a jiggle of my lantern to invite you to my future dances. This book was meant to be about Awareness... an entertaining and informative guide to Personality Development, Choice, Context, and Mood. Did we do it... you and I?

I hope that your interest has been tickled, and scratched, and massaged by the traces drawn here in the Sands of Time... and those marked by the hint of bear scat and chipmunk notes that Walt Kelly's Pogo and I poked at and daubed along the way... creating time-warp combinations, such as Greek Mythology's "Tantalus" with Lewis Carroll's "Frumious Bandersnatch." May the gentle winds of a well-paced enthusiasm caress your journey and fill the sails of your awareness for all the days of your life. Permit such terms as "vertical time" to excite your curiosity, rather than to put an ache in your trolley. Open wide the doors of your context and let the tides of change ebb and flow. Heck, take a chance! Learn some new dance steps.

"Uff da," by the way, according to E. C. "Red" Stangland in his Uff Da Jokes, "is more than an expression. Uff da defies precise definition. Anything from disappointment, sudden pain, surprised reactions to unexpected conditions are covered by the 'uff da' expression. It is also a philosophy that one doesn't have to swear, talk dirty, or blow a gasket. Uff da gives the signal that things are out of control for the moment, but the use of the expression surmounts the problem at hand." "Red" calls himself a FBN--Full Blooded Norsky--, who is, I expect, quite creative in his use of the "uff da" term. So no more whistling by the graveyard for me. From now on, I'll just say, "Uff da!"....

Good-bye remarks: May your journey be productive. Live actively. Expand your pyramid in all its dimensions. Do the creative dance. Be real. Be whole. Be as one with others and with Nature. And keep your eyes on the Eagle.

"If the universe is a uni-verse and if life is characterized by unity, then all things have relatedness and coordination," wrote Clarence R. Skinner in his Human Nature and the Nature of Evil. Mr C. went on to write, "As long as we care there is hope." and "Evil is that which prevents our fulfilling our best selves, whether it be an outward circumstance or inward condition."

"The earth," Walt Whitman said, "shall surely be complete to him or her who shall be complete.

The earth remains jagged and broken only to him or her who remains jagged and broken."

And while the beloved Satchel Paige advised, "Don't look back,'cause somethin' might be catchin' up." I seek his permission to add, "If you do look back, don't look back too long, 'cause you might run dead-wall into something."

Watch for my next "uff da" lantern to be hoisted up the Welcome Pole,.. and I will watch for yours. Now... finally... it's time for me to "manage-my-mood" outta' here. This book has been long enough in its birthin'.

Good night, Memphis Calabash. <u>Lebt wohl</u>. Make it a radiant, harmonious, wholesome, creative 21st Century, dear Terri Barton.

About the Author

Mike earned a Ph.D. in psychology about 25 years ago; in living he is still earning his wings. He believes that it is time to shell the nut of awareness,… and to move into the forum of the new century with chin up, head high, and eyes on the challenges that would thwart us from reaching for the greatness of our human potential. Mike is a flexible poet with no set meter, who believes in the positive possibilities of social networking. He was born in 1938 in West Virginia and he now lives in Idaho. He is interested in joining motivated others in creating a forum of awareness and energy for the mutual joy of opportunity, sharing, heart and dignity. Mike's lantern is up, and turns slowly in the winds of change and choice. Mike is contact friendly – try him.